Cinematic Coup de Grace
A Journey into the World of Cinema

Ryan S. Mudd

DEDICATION

For Kira and Max.
Your love, support, and help made this book possible.

CONTENTS

PART 1: REVIEWS

10 Cloverfield Lane

10 Cloverfield Lane is the spiritual successor to the film *Cloverfield*. While they are in the same fictional universe both movies can stand on their own independently. The acting in *10 Cloverfield Lane* is great and the isolated mood and scares are legitimate. The characters are interesting and have depth.

Michelle, played by Mary Elizabeth Winstead, has recently broken up with her fiancé. While driving through Louisiana she gets in a car accident. Michelle wakes up in the underground bunker of Howard, played by John Goodman. Howard nurses her wounds but won't let her out of the bunker. He tells her that there has been an attack and to leave the bunker would be certain death. Michelle has to determine if Howard is telling the truth or if he is just crazy and won't let her leave.

The actors all do an amazing job but the one that stood out the most was John Goodman. He is very realistic and scary as Howard. He pulls off a fantastic sociopath and it is a performance that makes the movie worth seeing. Mary Elizabeth Winstead is not just a damsel in distress and there are some tense moments that are very well performed.

The story in the bunker is very intense and the inclusion of Emmett, played by John Gallagher Jr. makes the dynamic between characters must more frightening. The ending almost seems like they changed to a different movie. This change did not make the movie bad but it also was not a huge surprise. The fact that this is a "Cloverfield" movie and attempting to be part of that franchise makes the ending less of a shock.

10 Cloverfield Lane is a fun movie that is certainly worth watching. It seems open to creating sequels. However, the idea of making stand alone films seems like a smart way to expand their universe. It is entertaining and creates feelings of tension that will have you talking long after the film has ended.

Ant-Man

With the Marvel Universe constantly expanding it is becoming more impressive what genres the studios are covering under the guise of superhero action films. With Captain America: The Winter Soldier audiences got a spy film and with Guardians of the Galaxy audiences were treated to a space action/comedy. With Ant-Man the superhero genre comes into a heist movie and it works really well.

Scott Lang, played by Paul Rudd, is a thief released from prison. Down on his luck and just wanting to have a relationship with his estranged daughter, he takes a burglary job to steal from Dr. Hank Pym, played by Michael Douglas. As it turns out the job was actually a challenge to see if he would be capable enough to steal some technology from Hank's former company. To assist in this venture Scott becomes the superhero, Ant-Man. He is capable of controlling ants mentally as well as shrinking to microscopic size and re-growing at will.

If this were a typical heist movie it would have fallen into cliché. However, since the element of superheroes is involved it makes the movie fresh and seems like a unique take on the genre. The action is fun to watch and the effects make it believable that this character can do the fantastic things he can do. There are some silly moments like a battle on a Thomas the Tank Engine train set that looks epic in small scale but like nothing when in normal size, but it adds to the entertainment as a whole.

The actors for the movie are all believable and likeable. Paul Rudd has clearly come a long way at his age to have a superhero body. Michael Douglas is also incredibly enjoyable as the first Ant-Man who experienced a great loss and has an estranged relationship with his daughter Hope, played by Evangeline Lilly. Corey Stroll is great as the villain. While we have seen him more as a jerk in a lot of other films, he portrays a lot of menace that comes off as threatening. It was also particularly nice to see Bobby Cannavale not cast as a jerk for a change.

Ant-Man is a unique movie that accepts its challenge to entertain and succeeds. There are so many brooding and dark themes in superhero movies and a fun heist movie is absolutely the new blood this genre needs. I completely recommend seeing this movie. It is a fun inclusion to the Marvel Universe and it will be great to see where this character goes in future features.

Arrival

Arrival has all the hallmarks of a good science fiction movie. It comes across as genuine, has great performances, and does not relish in over-blown special effects. However, it will be hard for anyone that is sensitive or finds themselves often empathizing with characters to enjoy this movie to its full potential. It can feel like a kick to the gut when you are expecting something more entertaining.

A dozen alien spacecraft have landed in various locations on Earth. Governments struggle to find out the aliens' intentions so they enlist the aid of linguist Louise Banks, played by Amy Adams. The aliens produce images to communicate, which require a lot of work to decipher and translate. Worldwide tensions mount as the different nations attempt to communicate but face a ticking clock that might lead to violence.

The good aspects of the movie are that the acting is great. Amy Adams and Jeremy Renner both deliver solid performances that show a lot of range. At no point did they take the easy route and make the movie seem emotionally manipulative. The movie is not muddled with cartoonish effects or eye candy. The alien space ship is a simple blank black metallic hallway. The creatures look like something that would result from the odd coupling of an Ent from *The Lord of the Rings* and the great race of Yith from the H.P. Lovecraft's mythos.

The story is captivating, though confusing at times. The introduction of a time spiral aspect took me out of the movie briefly as I fought to catch up to what was happening. Despite this, the movie has a solid flow that does not seem wasted on pointless padding. The awful nature of the twist ending is a mixture between bittersweet and damn tragic. The implications of it will leave audiences discussing the choices they would make in the characters' stead.

Arrival is a beautifully shot and well-acted film that displays all aspects of good science fiction. On the other hand, the emotional scenes can be difficult for certain audience members. A person should go into this movie expecting to feel emotionally drained when the lights go up at the conclusion. It is still entertaining, but that can be marred by the sheer force of the ending that hits like a two by four to the skull. To say it is not a good movie would be a disservice to the many people that really worked hard to make a good film, but to say the film will not depress the hell out of you would be an outright falsehood as well.

Avengers: Age of Ultron

I hate to say how disappointing this movie was. Sequels are rarely better than their predecessors and unfortunately this is case. It is not a bad film by any stretch, there is a bank of talent that is still trying to make a decent product, but as a whole the film is weaker than first but a vast margin. The first was impressive because it tied various directors, characters, and properties into a cohesive adventure. This feels like a long filler episode. This review may have some spoilers.

If you watched the events of *Iron Man 3* you might remember Iron Man getting surgery to have the shrapnel removed so that he is basically not Iron Man anymore. He destroyed all his suits and drove off to live happily as a billionaire. Well, Tony is back as Iron Man- no explanation there. What about the ending of *Thor 2* where we saw that Loki had taken over the throne of Asgard? Never even brought up. Instead of acknowledging the films that came before it like the first did, this movie seems to take great pains to avoid bringing them up.

Tony Stark, played by Robert Downey Jr. and Bruce Banner, played by Mark Ruffalo, create an artificial intelligence in the hopes that they can retire the Avengers and create a force for world peace. The AI-system is called

Ultron, voiced by James Spader, and he feels that the best way for there to be world peace is to destroy humanity. The Avengers must band together again to stop this robot menace and save the world.

Let's start by talking about what was good in this movie. James Spader is awesome as Ultron. His line delivery oozes with cold disgust for humanity and smug superiority. The other actors fall into their old rolls well and it is comfortable to see them again. The Scarlet Witch and Quicksilver have ridiculous accents that I personally could have done without, but both Aaron Taylor-Johnson and Elizabeth Olsen play their parts well.

The biggest problem to this movie is that there are too many characters to focus on. They have added several new characters and all deserve a backstory but all are basically glossed over. They instead focus on things that add nothing to the narrative, these include: discovery of Hawkeye's hidden family, the romance between Black Widow and the Hulk, Black Widow getting kidnapped by Ultron for no reason whatsoever, the trip to Africa, and the fight with the Hulk and the Hulkbuster. I would have gladly given those scenes up in order to have some character development. The action and CGI is fun to watch but after awhile I felt like I was just watching cartoon characters duke it out. The realism was just lost and it became even more silly than usual. Ultron's plan for the destruction of humanity is on par with a Bond villain and any amount of physics or logic should have made the plan implausible from the start. I guess they really wanted to make this comic movie seem like it was coming straight off the pages.

The worse offense is the obvious attempt to grasp at the audience's emotions. There is a character that dies in the film and his death is supposed to be big, dramatic, and meaningful. It would be if the audience cared who the character was. In the first film this was done when Agent Coulson was killed and he united the team in his death. Coulson had been in several other Marvel films and he was well liked. It was a shame when he died. This death just seemed empty and manipulative.

If you are a fan of the first Avengers movie you probably already brought your tickets to this blockbuster. If you are patient enough to wait then I recommend seeing it a rental. It's a good movie but it doesn't live up to the hype. An Avengers movie needs to be epic with things at stake and a narrative that isn't just a mass of quips and action scenes. This movie falls short where it could have been really unique and interesting. In making a series this epic, mediocrity can be one of the biggest crimes of all.

Batman v. Superman: Dawn of Justice

Acting as a sequel to the *Man of Steel* film, *Batman v. Superman: Dawn of Justice* is an introduction to the DC films: Batman, Wonder Women, and other members of the Justice League. Visually, it is a very pretty movie and the actors give it their best shot at making it entertaining. The problem is that the story is lackluster and the editing makes the movie difficult to watch.

Bruce Wayne, played by Ben Affleck, narrates his parents' death then flashes forward to Zod's attack on Metropolis where Bruce Wayne does whatever he can to save people. 18 months later Superman is still saving people while causing controversy and Batman has appeared in Gotham, stopping crimes with vigilante justice. The two figures do not agree with each other's methods of crime stopping so the villainous Lex Luthor is able to manipulate them into fighting each other.

The movie has some scenes that are lovely to look at; Superman saving a woman from a burning fire on the Day of the Dead or when he saves people on the roof of a house in a flood zone appearing like a floating angel above the people. These images create memorable moments that are impressive. Ben Affleck and Gal Gadot are a welcome add on to the film but feel under utilized. Ben Affleck spends most of his time looking angry and Gal Gadot spends most of her time wandering around looking pretty.

The casting of Lex Luthor is baffling. Jesse Eisenberg does bring a different mannerism to the character, coming off like a twitchy, nerdy, caricature of Mark Zuckerburg. At no point was his portrayal threating and he came off like a guy that was just angry that he was picked on in high school. The other odd casting choice is Jeremy Irons as Alfred. All previous portrayals of Alfred have been caring and smart but they were also Bruce Wayne's butler. In this film it is more confused as to Alfred's roll in Bruce's life. For example, Bruce even serves Alfred coffee in the morning.

The editing for this movie was a mess. There are more dream sequences then a Freddy Krueger film. There are scenes that even seem out of sequence of time that are not established and seem thoughtlessly put together. Even the character of Doomsday seems shoehorned in and looked like they were facing a cave troll from The Lord of the Rings movies. The fight scenes are fun to watch when you can see through the darkness.

The movie is very long and it takes a lot of time before any real action takes place. Meanwhile there are lots of shots of characters walking, brooding, and whining about one another. The other Justice League characters are introduced as well as foreshadowing of the threats they will face in the future. The movie adds these sections without explanation so it will likely fit together as new movies come out but as it is it is like having a puzzle with pieces that come in installments. All these parts might come together brilliantly one day but as the movie is it is very confusing as to what is dream and what is forecasting the future.

Batman v. Superman: Dawn of Justice is not a terrible movie but it is also not worth seeing in theaters. It is too long of a sit and not as thought out as it should have been. It is obvious that DC wants to have the same success as Marvel in their cinematic universe. The big difference that is working for Marvel is that it took its time putting out solo movies first to create an established universe before putting the heroes together as a team. With DC it feels like a big game of catch-up that is very rough and not nearly as entertaining as the individual films. *Batman v. Superman: Dawn of Justice* is a grim movie that will likely scare many audiences from future DC movies.

B.C. Butcher

B.C. Butcher is the kind of film that seems like it was fun to be on the set. That same fun is not felt in the overall production. The story is muddled, the effects are terrible, the script is childish, and the acting is groan-worthy. I can excuse a lot since the writer-director was a child herself when writing and directing this film. *B.C. Butcher* is a piece of clay in search of a sculptor. It will likely entertain a very select group of tastes.

Neandra, a cave woman and leader of her tribe gets jealous of a girl who was with her caveman, Rex, played by Kato Kaelin. Neandra sacrifices this girl on a tree and the B.C. Butcher, a monster that lives in the area, apparently finds the body and puts it upon himself to enact revenge upon the women that killed the girl. Can Neandra stop this monster?

The music in this movie is good. There is a punk/rockabilly vibe that is sort of reminiscent of a 1960s movie, which is stylized and cool. The script is mostly filled with pre-historical puns like an episode of *The Flintstones*. At times it is clever and at times it will make you roll your eyes. There is a vibe that this would be the tribe that Bettie Page would be in when she was in her tribal garb.

The costumes are simply leopard print cloth torn to look like loincloths. The monster is so obviously a guy in a bad mask that he might as well have been a trick-or-treater that walked on the set. They use clearly anachronistic items like steak knives, sunglasses, and have metal piercings. The title character is also called B.C. Butcher. I find that perplexing as that means that cave people have knowledge of the difference between BC/AD and also have somehow figured out the profession of butcher. Normally, I do not try to nitpick that sort of thing to such a degree but when it takes me out the movie it should be brought up. Not that this movie seems to desire to keep its audience in the movie. For example: apropos of nothing there is a scene in which the director's boyfriend, Rodney Bingenheimer, shows up in modern dress with a duck to introduce a band that plays.

B.C. Butcher is like watching a teenage girl's home movie. You are impressed that they made something but you also feel a bit embarrassed for the people involved. The good thing is that the sound track is tolerable and the movie is short. It is campy and I suppose a person can enjoy it for that quality as well. The worst aspect is Kato Kalein. In an interview it stated that much of his dialogue was improvised. I am sure he is a nice guy, but his jokes simply do not land and he comes off like a kid trying so hard to make a group of adults laugh. His character could have almost been written out and the film would have been better for it.

B.C. Butcher unfortunately is just not entertaining enough to recommend to people. It feels like the results of a slumber party and too much sugar. There are so many better caveman movies out there. If you are looking for something serious go with *Quest For Fire* if you are looking for lighter fare I suggest *One Million Years B.C.* Director, Kansas Bowling is still very young and has a long career ahead of her. The movie is flawed but it looks like it was fun to make and I imagine that if you are a fan of cute girls in leopard print and movies that are so corny that they feel like they come right off the kernel, than this film might be right off your alley. It is a Troma production and with that comes a certain quality you need to be prepared to experience.

Big Eyes

When Tim Burton has the right project he can accomplish great things. This film takes a look at a repressed artist and displays it with elaborate colors and big performances. Amy Adams is in top form for her performance as Margaret

Keene.

Margaret Keene, played by Amy Adams, is a '50s suburban housewife who leaves her husband in an attempt to gain some freedom in her life. She meets and falls in love with Walter, played by Christoph Waltz. Margaret's paintings become successful but Walter takes credit for them. This causes much turmoil and eventually ruins their marriage. Amy Adams is great at portraying the stereotypical '50s housewife. She looks repressed and the pain on her face is evident in nearly every shot. The lies she tells to keep up this ruse are truly tearing her up inside. Christoph Waltz plays a great sneaky con man. His snake-oil salesman grin is perfect for the role and at no time did I think he didn't believe his own hype. The only thing I would have toned down was the courtroom scene. In that scene Walter's character goes from sophisticated con man to clownish fool.

The movie itself is beautiful. There are so many colors on screen it was sometimes hard to believe it was a Tim Burton film. Another cool effect were people cast in small roles with larger eyes. For example, Krysten Ritter. I am not sure if that was by design or if the make-up department made it obvious that eyes were important in the movie. It was hard not to notice them.

I would recommend this movie to anyone who likes an underdog story. It is a good movie despite some hi-jinx by Waltz. The story of an artist wanting to be recognized for her work in a world that basically kept her silent is worth telling. It has some great performances and stunning visuals. It is certainly worth a matinee viewing at the very least.

Blair Witch

The Blair Witch Project is a creepy movie that has a very genuine feel to it. The sequel entitled *Blair Witch*, attempts to market on the first film's charm but misses all of the aspects that made it successful. It was as if the makers of the movie asked themselves what made the original film memorable and just replied "the woods and motion-sickness inducing photography." The characters are forgettable and the scares resort to jump and gross-outs.

James Donahue, the younger brother of Heather from the first film, sees some footage online which makes him believe that his sister is still alive in the Black Hills forest. This is despite that it would mean she survived for 16 years hidden from search teams. James and a group of his friends go into the woods to see if they can unravel the mystery. Once they get into the woods strange things begin happening and they find themselves a part of the horrors of the Blair Witch.

When you consider that the first film was improvised, filmed on a tiny budget, and didn't show much of the scares, it is amazing that it stands up as a legitimate horror film today. *Blair Witch* has the aspect of being lost in the woods but with the same jump scare clichés that could be found in your everyday horror film. This could be forgiven if the characters were interesting or memorable in anyway, but they are one-dimensional caricatures that are disposable.

The biggest crime is that the film considers itself a *Blair Witch* movie but does create tension built on what you don't see. Even Book of Shadows: Blair Witch 2 got this aspect right. The deaths are shown and even the Blair Witch makes an appearance looking like the creature at the end of *Quarantine* but with sound effects of one of the Ents from *The Lord of the Rings* movies. The filmmakers resort to loads of the same jump scares that were popular in the 1980s. Why make a movie like this if you cannot even capture the aspects that made the first movie popular? Blair Witch is a missed opportunity to make a modern twist on a spooky movie that comes off like an American legend. It fails to deliver anything new and will likely be forgotten in time. I only slightly recommend it, and only if you are a fan of the original, and only as a rental. This movie makes Book of Shadows: Blair Witch 2 seems like a smart movie in comparison. It is another case of banking on nostalgia to sell movie tickets to mediocrity.

Captain America: Civil War

Coming in as the lucky 13th film in the Marvel Cinematic Universe *Captain America: Civil War* is a fun and fresh story featuring a host of the Avengers we have grown to love as well as some new characters to the roster. The movie as a whole is not as bold as past Captain America films but the action is solid and the return of characters keep the pulse of this movie moving strong.

Captain America/Steve Rogers, played by Chris Evans, and some of the Avengers are stopping some terrorists in Lagos. Unfortunately, in the processes several innocent people are killed. This leads the United Nations to decide that the Avengers must register with them as a governing body overseeing their actions. Iron Man/Tony Stark, played by Robert Downey Jr., welcomes this change to be held more accountable. Captain America feels that governing bodies will always have agendas and he does not want to be told who to help and who not to help. Both heroes gain supporters which lead to debate, anger, and eventual blows from both sides of the issue.

The action is fun to watch and the characters play their parts well. The addition of T'Challa/Black Panther, played by Chadwick Boseman, Peter Parker/Spider-man, played by Tom Holland, and Helmut Zemo, played by Daniel Bruhl are welcome additions. It was also very entertaining to see Paul Rudd reprise his role as Scott Lang/Ant-man. To see the characters work well with one another in such fantastic battles really made the movie a solid popcorn flick.

The few complaints I have about the movie are nitpicking things. The stakes could have (and honestly should have been) much higher at this point. There could have been more development to the new characters; however, this is a Captain America movie so the focus really should be on him and his conflict with the Winter Soldier and Iron Man. If anything, this movie probably could have been a third Avengers film but because of the story focus it is easy to understand why it went in this direction. It was bizarre to have an Avengers movie where Thor and the Hulk are absent.

Captain America: Civil War is an entertaining new addition to the Marvel Cinematic Universe. If you are looking for a great summer blockbuster give this movie a try. It is exciting and not nearly as dark as some of the past Captain America films. You are sure to enjoy the acting and action playing together in a wild spectrum of comic book intensity. If you are a comic book fan or a fan of the other films this movie will not disappoint.

Cherry Falls

Cherry Falls is a satirical slasher film that seems like it is built for cult status. The story is silly, as many slasher movies tend to be. Still, the actors at least try to make the humor subtle without going into a meta territory like *Scream* or winking at the camera like later *Nightmare on Elm St.* movies. The gravitas that the main actors bring make the movie interesting and watchable.

Cherry Falls is a town in Virginia where teenagers are being brutally murdered. Their dead bodies have the word "virgin" carved into them. As Jody Marken, played by Brittany Murphy, goes to school and find out about the fate of her fellow students, she soon finds herself being chased by the killer. The killer creates a scare in the community where all the virgins want to loose their virginity so that they will not be targets of the killer's rage.

For the most part the actors are the standard teenage slasher movie tropes. Hordes of twenty-somethings pretending to be teenagers acting like stupid stereotypes. You do not care if they die because they are painfully annoying. Brittany Murphy, Michael Biehn, and Jay Mohr are actually trying to make an entertaining movie and anything entertaining coming out of it is almost solely owed to their talents. The many other characters could easily be replaced by cartoon characters with names like "gay best friend," "slutty friend," and "loud-mouth bully." Brittany Murphy was an underrated actress who will certainly be missed. Her performance is vulnerable and believable despite the rather ludicrous material. Michael Biehn is sort of under utilized. He is the sheriff and Brittany Murphy's father in the film. He is trying to make the script work for him but at times he seems like he is just annoyed with people. However, since he is playing an overworked sheriff, that attitude seems to work. Jay Mohr is great. His acting range goes from a subtle, calm one to a scenery-chewing ten.

The movie is said to have gone through five attempts to the MPAA before the censors would approve it. That being said, it would have been so interesting to see a director's cut of this movie. It does feel like there might have been a lot more gore and sex at one point but it was neutered for a more mainstream audience. It is the sort of movie that should draw a cult status form fans of horror that is not that serious or scary.

The story is silly. The overall motivation of the killer is mindless. It is a tale of revenge but it is also chaotic and directionless. Much like Ghost Face from *Scream*, the killer spends a great deal of time placing his victims in scary positions and getting his butt-kicked by the protagonist. The teens discussing losing their virginity to save their lives is amusing and the inevitable orgy that ensues is laughable but makes the movie at least unique.

The movie is full of product placement for Coca Cola and other junk food. Not to the point of distraction, but many shots linger on desk or tables with Coke products. The movie does not seem to take itself too seriously but it also does not go to the level of being so over-the-top that it comes off like the characters are winking at the camera or just going through the motions to get their paycheck.

Cherry Falls is worth checking out. If you are a horror fan or a slasher movie fan then this movie will entertain you. The film is just unique enough to not fall into the same camp as the horde of movies that came out during the *Scream* generation of horror movies. The great performances really make this hidden gem into something that hopefully finds more of an audience in a cult status and the ending kicks the movie into an insane gear, which will have the audience laughing at how over-the-top things get.

Choose Their Kill – A New Venue For Retro Humor Horror

CryptTV, the digital studio co-founded by director Eli Roth, recently released the YouTube sensation, *Choose Their Kill*. Directed by Standards of Living director Aaron Mento, *Choose Their Kill* is a "choose-your-own-adventure" style of digital series. All choices feature colorful characters and over-the-top deaths, which make for a fun watch.

The scenarios primarily revolve around a mime, a fitness nut, or a green energy icon going about their daily business when someone does something that annoys them. The viewer is then presented with some options on how to dispose of this annoyance. There is an option to spare the person, however, that person usually meets a grim fate nonetheless.

This is a really fun series with good acting and a great concept behind it. I imagine there will be a lot of great ideas down the pipeline as director Aaron Mento is a very creative writer/director. If you are a fan of odd and dark humor this will certainly be up your alley. The videos can be found now on CryptTV's YouTube Channel:

https://www.youtube.com/watch?v=FPwJTNaDDuQ&list=PLfarU_76noqqLsnTLM4oXk2C3_v-L9eHN.

Creed

After the previous film in the *Rocky* series I was sure that the story of Rocky Balboa was wrapped up tighter than a snare drum. I was dead wrong. A cleverly written story encapsulating all the heart of the original characters and bringing a new life to the franchise I can see Adonis Creed as a people's champion for a new generation. The acting is great and the story is fantastic. Considering this is the first of the *Rocky* series to not be written by Sylvester Stallone, it feels like his hand is certain involved in the spirit of things.

Adonis "Donnie" Creed, played by Michael B. Jordan is the bastard son of Apollo Creed. After finding out his who his father is, he attempts to make a name for himself in the boxing world. He goes to Tijuana and wins a few fights and finds that he needs a trainer if he will ever move up the ranks in the boxing ring. Adonis enlists the aid of Apollo's greatest rival Rocky Balboa to train him.

If there were anything bad about this movie it would only be small, nitpicking stuff. For example: No one ever mentions Ivan Drago as the guy who killed Apollo Creed in *Rocky IV*. No one ever discusses the failed time Rocky trained Tommy Gunn in *Rocky V*. I could really piss and moan about how Rocky isn't more famous after his exhibition match in *Rocky Balboa* with Mason "The Line" Dixon. It is hard to be upset though when this is the same series where a robot with artificial intelligence was given to Paulie for his birthday. Pick your battles.

The movie has all the feel of a *Rocky* movie. The main character is charming and is believable as Apollo Creed's son. Rocky is still as strong-hearted and good-natured person. The cast does a great job bringing this underdog story home. Once again creating a believable task and facing a "villain" that is not bad but merely an antagonist in every sense of the word. I would not be shocked if Stallone was nominated for best supporting actor come Oscar season.

I would recommend, first and foremost, if you decide to watch this movie that at least see the previous films. The previous films will give you insight on who everyone is or was. *Creed* is worth seeing, especially if you are a fan of the Rocky series. *Creed* is a welcome addition and was clearly written by someone that knows the characters and loves the material. See it if you can.

Deadly Famous

Deadly Famous is a 2014 documentary style horror movie. The acting is borderline insane and the story is non-existent. While the story is ludicrous, there are some funny moments that come out of nowhere. These moments are not enough to save the film from being fairly forgettable. The movie begins as if it is a documentary about Alan Miller. Alan is a former child star that has a penchant for killing young women. Living in Hollywood he has a plethora of possible victims. We see Alan's footage as he frequently uses his camera during his murders. He finds a young woman that becomes his roommate. She becomes famous and finds love on the set of a Soap Opera, which enrages Alan.

The funny thing about Alan is that people do not seem notice that he is clearly psychotic. He finds girls from Craig's List and, instead of being put off by the fact that he films everything, he picks up girls from the street too. He is a clearly unhinged character and anyone with a functioning brain would avoid this raving, manic nut. At the very least, a normal person would have called the police after being harassed by him.

There are a few aspects that are impressive about this movie. The photography is beautiful. There are scenes where the background views from the Hollywood hills are the highpoint. The tone shifts are sometimes awkward. For example, there is a scene of Alan and his friend at the Santa Monica boardwalk and it is filmed beautifully. It then cuts to a shot of Alan masturbating furiously.

The beginning credits sequence is a lot like the ones from the film *Se7en* but with photos of real victims of serial killers like the Black Dahlia. Many other scenes like the masturbation ones can take the audience out of the film. It is difficult to imagine that people would feel the need to film themselves awkwardly masturbating or that killing people would have be filmed in multiple angels from the same camera. The cameo performance of Eric Roberts was a delight and sadly not utilized fully. Roberts plays a caricature of himself where he spends a great deal of his screen time high on cocaine.

The story is a bit perplexing. There is nothing that is keeping it in the documentary style and the movie only uses that framework at the beginning and end of the film. One scene is a couple at the pond looking for their dog. It makes me wonder what couple goes looking for their dog at the pound and feel the compulsion to film it. There are a number of victims that escape Alan and it makes me wonder how he has not been caught yet.

The effects are not really well done. The blood comes off looking a lot more like Kool-Aid and the makeup seemed comically unreal. In one scene a girl is supposed to look like she has had half of her face scarred with cuts. Instead it looks like a latex mess. The blood stains on the wall look like a little child threw their cup of V-8 on the wall.

Alan is not a compelling protagonist. Even as killer he is racist, abrasive, and creepy. He just roams Hollywood, looking slouchy and creepily watching women. Only the dumbest girls fall for his trap and basically let him kill them. They go against all the smart things that people do to keep themselves safe. They get in his car, come to his house, and even let him touch them without leaving immediately.

Deadly Famous is not something I can recommend to people. It lacks a basic plot and the main character is very dislikable. Still, if you are an Eric Roberts fan you might glean some enjoyment out the film. Considering the strange tone of the film it might have been better had it been written as an irreverent comedy or a satirical movie mocking the genre. There are many other serial killer movies that are much more memorable.

Deadpool

Deadpool is about the anti-hero from Marvel comics, which has a certain place in a lot of fans' hearts because of his dark humor and violence. The problem is that the plot is not very interesting. There is no huge threat that makes the movie memorable or has elements of threat. *Deadpool* basically takes one interesting character and places him in a story that is not a huge deal.

Wade Wilson/Deadpool, played by Ryan Reynolds is a mercenary that was disfigured after a medical test gave him super human healing. He spends his days trying to find the man responsible and hopefully cure his disfigurement. All the while a great deal of his time is spent telling his story and breaking the fourth wall in a comedic fashion.

Ryan Reynolds is great in the part of Deadpool. The filmmakers did a great job making it seem like the character is straight off the pages of the comics. The problem is that the story line is not anything worth mentioning. The main conflict in the story would have easily been remedied by a simple conversation with his girlfriend. It is basically a sitcom scenario that results in hundreds of dead guys.

There are a few funny moments where Deadpool makes note of the casting of the movie or even makes note of superhero movie tropes. The problem is that the rest of the dialog is nearly all dick and fart jokes. This makes me think that maybe this movie was made for a bit of a younger crowd. However, this movie is rated R so I am not sure what demographic this movie is supposed to appeal to in the audience.

Deadpool is an okay movie. It plays it safe though and does not take a lot of risks with the story. The movie is basically a chance to make up for the Deadpool character being so poorly written in the Wolverine movie. It had potential, but Ryan Reynold's charm can't carry this movie alone. If they make a sequel I can hope that they cast people that work to make a coherent story with some depth.

Dementia

Dementia is a 2015 psychological horror movie that showcases some great acting. The story is okay but contains characters that are both interesting and flawed. The story occasionally requires some suspension of disbelief to make it function for the viewer. There were also a few technical aspects that made the film difficult to watch, but despite the minor flaws, it is a good movie that shows talent of all the individuals involved.

George Lockhart, played by Gene Jones, is an elderly Vietnam vet. One day he suffers a stroke and is told by doctors that he suffers from dementia. A nurse visits his home while George is recovering and George's son and granddaughter hire her to stay and assist. The nurse is a young woman named Michelle, played by Kristina Klebe, who takes advantage of George's health problems to exact a sinister revenge plot. George's granddaughter, played Hassie Harrison, thinks something is amiss and investigates.

The acting for this movie is really well done. Gene Jones, Kristina Klebe, and Hassie Harrison give standout performances. Gene Jones is great at displaying his range from sad and vulnerable to enraged and sinister. Kristina Klebe goes from sweet and caring to sinister and menacing in a very believable fashion. Hassie Harrison's character has the most obvious character arc, going from uncaring to caring and then disillusioned. The casting is great and other characters really fit well into their roles, making the central figures to the story seem better rounded. The film seems to have elements of *What Ever Happened to Baby Jane?* with twists that make it subtly unique.

There are a few technical aspects that made this film difficult to watch. The night shots are almost too dark at times making the movie difficult to see. The soundtrack is eerie but is also so loud at times that the dialogue is difficult to make out what is being said. The rest of the film is really well made and shows a great deal of skill in making some of the nightmarish qualities come together perfectly.

The story seemed like it could have been developed in more detail. I am not a fan of killing an animal character to make the antagonist seem truly evil. The movie carries the plot in a natural flow but the revelations at the conclusion make it feel a bit rushed. It also felt like the conclusion felt hollow. This was due to the fact that throughout the film we are watching the granddaughter and George become closer through their ordeal and then it is essentially destroyed when you find out the dark secret that ties Michelle to George. On the plus side, the revelation is subtle and there are clues all over to point to it so it does not come off something completely out of left field. The actors at least seemed to take their roles seriously and their range of skills is put to the test.

A person being tormented by their caretaker is not a particularly new plot development. *Dementia* at least takes this aspect and adds enough unique qualities that the movie does not come off as rote. Most of the characters seem to have a solid arc that make the movie thrilling at times. The revenge motivation is a bit muddled but it fits enough that it does not come off like a M. Night Shyamalan style twist. The bottom line is that the story seems to say that all people pay the price for their misdeeds in the end. *Dementia* is worth looking into if you are looking for something different. The solid acting is entertaining and very real given the rough trip the story takes you on. It is a dark movie about a dark subject matter and the mood is appropriate to the tone of the film. The aspects to this move that are flawed are fairly minimal and the high points of the acting really make this movie stick out.

Don't Breathe

Conceptually, *Don't Breathe* is a scary idea. The movie is replete with tension, complete with occasional jump scares and camera angles that build up on the fear. The acting is also very good, making the antagonist of the film seem both pitiable and deranged. If there is one flaw to this movie is that the writing made the protagonist unbelievably stupid and fairly unlikable given her motivation.

Rocky, played by Jane Levy, Alex, and Money are three criminals that make a living breaking into homes in Detroit. Rocky has an abusive, alcoholic mother so she is desperate for money to get her and her sister moved to California. Money hears of a blind veteran who is supposed to have $300,000 stashed at his house. The gang pack up and attempt to rob the blind man. Little do they know that just because he is blind, he is far from being as helpless as they imagined.

Jane Levy does a great job acting scared. She is not the most likable character but when she is on screen you can believe that she thinks she is going to die. The blind man, played by Stephen Lang, is also believable. His performance was like a mix of his past performances ranging from pathetic Ike Clanton from *Tombstone* to his angry badass role as Colonel Quaritch, from *Avatar*. There are times when I was disgusted by his character's insanity but also pitied him for what brought him to that state.

I am not a burglar. My knowledge of breaking and entering is limited to: Don't do it. These characters have been at this a long time but still seem so dumb. They talk loudly, they leave enough evidence to fill an entire crime lab, they do not plan beyond face value, and they do not know when to leave. Just adding the motivation for Rocky to leave her abusive household is not enough to make her altruistic in my eyes. She could get a job and move out of her Mom's place and call Child Protective Services on her mother.

Despite its shortfalls, *Don't Breathe* is great at building tension. The camera often focuses on just the character's face so that the audience cannot see what is coming behind the corner or they won't notice something fast moving until it is too late. The darkness plays its own role in the film, keeping you on edge until the end.

Don't Breathe is a flawed but good movie. The ending felt a bit hollow as there was no catharsis and it has a bitter feeling of evil winning with no lesson learned. It is certainly worth renting and possibly worth a matinee if you are a horror fan. *Don't Breathe* would be a great companion movie with *Hush*, which came out recently as well. The thrills are legitimate and will have you leaving the theater with pieces of chair stuck under your nails from griping the seat.

Ex Machina

The sci-fi genre is rife with films that query about the

wisdom of creating computers with functioning artificial intelligence. *Ex Machina* seems to ask a lot of valid questions regarding the Turing test when it comes to the nature of programmable behavior. It is a smart film that has some great ideas and will have you pondering long after the movie is over.

Caleb, played by Domhall Gleeson, wins a lottery to spend a week with the CEO of *Bluebook*, a fictional search engine. He is greeted by Nathan, played by Oscar Isaac, who tells him he has created an android with near perfect AI and he needs Caleb to perform a Turing test on her. The Turing test is a test, which is used when an interrogator is needed to ask questions of a person to determine whether they are a human or computer. The android, Ava, played by Alicia Vikander, meets Caleb and soon develops a strong friendship with him.

The psychology of this movie is fascinating. I couldn't help but wonder what questions I would ask to determine what makes a human truly human. The philosophical nature bleeds into a psychological story when we realize that some characters might not be as truthful as others and Ava is not the first android to be built. The acting is great and the small cast really utilizes their relationships together to make this a compelling film. Oscar Isaac in particular is intimidating and yet also the sort of person who has a magnetic personality. The set is also interesting because there is a huge contrast between the home of Nathan, which is bare of nearly all décor and the land surrounding it since it is around some of the most scenic glaciers, forests, and waterfalls.

Ex Machina is a heavy movie. If you are into sci-fi with

some content that will lead to conversations then this is for sure a movie you will enjoy. If you are into lighter films or movies with heavy action then it is probably good to give it a pass. There are just some existential questions you will be coming to terms with at some point.

From Hell

From Hell is a 2001 movie that tells the story of the Jack the Ripper murders. The film is loosely based on the graphic novel by Alan Moore and Eddie Campbell and follows the character of Fredrick Abberline as the films protagonist. *From Hell* is an interesting interpretation of the Jack the Ripper story going into Royal conspiracy and building on an atmosphere of gory legend. Much like the source material, the movie does a good job transporting the audience to the location of Whitechapel England in the Victoria era.

Mary Kelly, played by Heather Graham, is a prostitute in Whitechapel England. She and a group of prostitute friends go about their day to day drudgery when one them is kidnapped. Then, one-by-one, they are murdered in horrific fashion by a murderer known as Jack the Ripper. It is up to inspector Fredrick Abberline, played by Johnny Depp, to catch the killer before more innocents can be killed. Soon they are drawn into a conspiracy involving Freemasons and the Royal Family.

From Hell is a beautiful movie. The filmmakers did a wonderful job capturing the grim world of Victorian era England. The camera work and stylized shots are very artistic and really make the movie seem dark and deep with a sort of nightmarish essence through every shot. There are numerous references to the fact that this is the Victorian era. Things like a Buffalo Bill Wild West Show pamphlet or having John Merrick, The Elephant Man, make a cameo appearance might seem clever on paper but on screen it takes you out of the movie. It felt like these sorts of additions were there simply to hit the audience over the head with the time period.

Heather Graham is noticeably bad in this movie. Her cockney accent is not on point at all and she seems to be struggling with portraying basic human emotions. Johnny Depp is not much better as he mumbles in a sleepwalker's haze through his performance. This movie owes much to the talent of the character actors that make this movie watchable. Robbie Coltrane, Ian Holm and Jason Flemyng all give dynamite performances that pick up the slack that the leads cannot seem to carry.

The story itself is intriguing enough but there is very little reason for the lead characters to even be present. For some reason Fredrick Abberline is a psychic. This seems pointless as this ability does not allow him to save anyone from Jack the Ripper and it does not lead to him catching the killer. In fact the killer, once questioned, confesses everything in a greatly over-the-top fashion makes the visions Abberline have even more bizarre. Also the killer goes from zero to psychotic in seconds flat. There was no telling as to why the insane switch was pulled, but when it was the killers eyes go black and he rambles insane nonsense as if he is evil personified, which is a touch out of character but it is nevertheless entertaining to watch.

The romance between Abberline and Mary is forced at best and the conclusion that is derived from it is not earned. It felt like a needlessly tacked on happy ending. Even the details of Abberline's previous marriage and his wife's death seemed like subjects that were tacked on to emotionally manipulate the audience rather than create a fleshed out character. It would have preferred they leave him out completely if they cannot make a character that is developed beyond a cop with a chip on his shoulder.

From Hell is a good movie for a rental. It showcases a creepy atmosphere and scenes that are gritty and haunting. While the effects are dated and a bit silly, it is still one of the better movies featuring the subject of Jack the Ripper. The conspiracy sort of falls apart if you take a moment to think about it. It is still an entertaining movie that has a gothic feel that will linger with you days after viewing.

Ghostbusters (2016)

The idea of a reboot of *Ghostbusters* did not thrill me. When I saw the commercial it looked gimmicky and screamed "cash-grab." Still, I went in hoping for the best from this movie that stared a group of funny women and headed by a competent comedic director. The movie is okay but flawed. There are some funny moments that make the film likable but they are marred by an underwhelming story and poorly written characters.

Dr. Erin Gilbert, played by Kristin Wiig, is a physics teacher attempting to gain tenure. A former book she published with Dr. Abby Yates, played by Melissa McCarthy, is causing problems with her credibility. When Gilbert confronts Yates they team up with engineer Holtzmann, played by Kate McKinnon, to investigate a haunted mansion. Upon discovery of the ghost, they work to trap the spiritual entities. Patty Tolan, played by Leslie Jones, an MTA worker that has witnessed the paranormal first hand, eventually joins them. Together they must face an evil nerd who wants to create an undead apocalypse.

In the original film, the Ghostbusters had quirky personality types that play well against a world that plays it straight through the film. In the Paul Feig *Ghostbusters* world everybody is quirky so the main characters need to be VERY quirky. This aspect comes off a bit annoying. The character of Holtzmann was painful to watch. This was disappointing since McKinnon is amazing on SNL. The secretary Kevin, played by Chris Hemsworth, is hunky and over-the-top stupid. Considering that *Ghostbusters* has a very strong girl power message it felt out of place by having Erin drool over the pretty but incompetent secretary.

The acting was enjoyable. Abby and Erin do their parts well but the character of Patty was surprisingly good. She was upbeat and the character was not too intense. The evil nerd that causes all the spiritual mischief is amusing as well, though his motivation was a bit trite. He is basically evil because he was picked on. The idea of a vexed, angry geek is a lot less threating than a Babylonian god. There are many cameos, which sometimes work well and fit into the plot and other times take you out of the movie by knocking you on the head as if saying "Remember *Ghostbusters!*"

As a whole this version of *Ghostbusters* is okay. It might be worth a rental if you are really curious. It is not nearly the caliber of the original. It feels a lot more like an SNL sketch that was stretched for time. It has moments that make it enjoyable but it still comes off as a gimmicky as a concept as *Blues Brothers 2000.* If the mood "meh" had a face it might look like the reboot of *Ghostbusters*.

Hell and Back

Just when you thought the worst thing that Freestyle Releasing put out was *God's Not Dead*, along came a fancy new contender, *Hell and Back*. Had I been in middle school or possibly high on drugs, this might have been a humorous movie. Sadly, the tone of the humor was lost on me and I did not feel anything more than relief at seeing the credits roll. It is a damn shame since it involves a lot of talented individuals and the animation is lively. On paper this sounds like an entertaining project but on screen it is devoid of fun and feels like a joyless slog.

Three foul-mouthed friends, Curt, Augie, and Remy work at a failing carnival. Curt makes a blood oath with Satan and because he does not take it seriously it is broken minutes later, leaving Curt to suffer the consequences. Curt is sucked into a vortex into hell and it is up to Augie and Remy to get Curt back from the denizens of Hell. With the help of a sexy half-breed demon and a Greek hero, Augie and Remy attempt to thwart the devil and return back on Earth.

The animation is pretty solid. It should always be commendable when movies take the time to put in the work for stop motion. The voice talents are tremendous and it is as though someone picked up a Hollywood phonebook and found every comedian possible to cast in this movie for even the most trivial of parts. Unfortunately, these factors do not make a good movie.

The story is fairly predictable and offers nothing new to the viewer. The jokes are stale and would only amuse a middle school student or an immature personality. Normally I find humor in the right sex joke, fat joke, and rape joke, but these were so generic and cliché that they missed the mark. The characters are all very unlikable and do not do anything beyond their stereotypes for the sake of development. For example: Augie is the one-dimensional fat character. That is all he is and all he is known for. Most of his gags are about his weight and at no point does his character grow or learn how to cope with his issues. He is simply the fat guy and that is all he will remain. Remy on the other hand is just an unlikeable jerk that hates everyone and treats his friends like crap. He learns nothing and is rewarded for his stupidity.

Considering that the minds behind *Robot Chicken* are involved with this I really had higher expectations. The jokes on that show are relevant to many pop culture scenarios, which could be considered funny. *Hell and Back* just says as many swear words as possible in the hopes that it will shock a laugh out of you. Often resulting in silent failure. The jokes do not allow for build up and pay off but rather to throw as much fast-pitch stupidity as possible at the audience to see what sticks.

I cannot recommend this movie for a rental. The subject material is too infantile for adults and too adult for kids. Why would they add sentient trees that rape people? The only reason I can figure is that someone thought that it was a bizarre way to be edgy. That could have been a perfect time for an *Evil Dead* joke, instead the joke implies that the guy is asking to be raped because he was dressed "like a bush." If the failed jokes in this movie saved lives, there would be no need for hospitals. It is not a fun movie and it certainly is not funny enough to spend time on. Save your money and save your time not watching this heartless drivel. If you want a stop motion movie with some brains and heart I recommend the 2009 *Mary and Max*. It might not be the trip into hell you were expecting but at least it is worth your time.

Hush

Hush is a horror movie from director Mike Flanagan. The thrills are genuine and the acting is fantastic. The film takes home invasion genre and pushes new life into it with the addition of a character that is deaf and mute. Like Oculus and Absentia, it creates elements of unease and terror that will impress even the most cynical critic.

Maddie Young, played by Kate Siegel, is a young deaf writer living in an isolated cottage in the woods. As she works on her latest novel a masked killer attacks her neighbor. Unable to hear the screams, she attracts the attention of the killer who attempts to break into the house and kill Maddie. Maddie must find a way to successfully hide, run, or fight back.

Kate Siegel does amazing work as Maddie. She is personable and charismatic so you really want her to live through this frightening ordeal. There is very little dialogue so the movie relies a lot on her physical performance and it pays off. The atmosphere and the unnerving factor of Maddie's handicap make the character very unique.

The movie is not shy on violence. The gore comes off as very realistic and appropriate to the mood of the story. We never find out the killer's motivation, which makes it all the more terrifying. Maddie is not written as a typical damsel and her vulnerability makes the performance very realistic and human. The killer is scary and does not fall into the cliché of the mindless slasher or the smart mouthed witty murder. The movie is a living chess game between killer and victim and as the audience we are watching the wheels turn in both their heads and hoping that Maddie will survive.

The movie takes the slasher genre in a bold new direction and is absolutely worth seeing. The acting and direction come together perfectly to make a movie that is sure to become a horror classic. This movie is a must see for any horror fan or anyone who wants to see a movie that is truly thrilling and interesting to behold.

Independence Day: Resurgence

Independence Day: Resurgence is the sequel to the 1996 summer blockbuster. Where the previous film was a fun and silly movie that invited audiences to shut off their brains and enjoy the action, this sequel feels rushed and lacks all of the charm of the original. The dialogue is laughable, the characters are underdeveloped, and the tone is all over the map.

Twenty years after the events of the Independence Day the world has changed drastically. Victory over the alien invaders has led to near world peace and reverse engineering of the alien technology has led to a revolution in mechanics. Having received the previous invader's distress call, the alien menace has returned with new weapons searching for an object that could lead to their undoing.

The concept of a peaceful world with almost futuristic technology was very cool. Unfortunately, the idea is squandered since the characters are not well developed and have dialogue that could be found in a comic book. Will Smith is greatly missed, as they seem to attempt to fill the void with characters we do not care about and comic relief that is not funny. The deaths in this movie lack any gravitas and have not earned the dramatic mood they attempted to achieve.

There should have been a twist ending to this movie where it turns out it was all in the mind of a child playing with toys. Instead the audience is treated to sequel bait that nobody could possibly care about with the exception of the actors needing the paycheck. It has all the touches of a Roland Emmerich without any charm and could have been a direct to video movie. The basic concept and some of the effects are fun to watch but without solid acting, a story, or even decent dialogue the film feels like a hollow cash-in.

Innocent Blood

Innocent Blood is a horror/comedy directed by John Landis. The performances in this movie are played straight for the most part which makes the movie a fun and entertaining story to watch. It is a movie that requires a certain element of having an open mind so that you can enjoy the ludicrous nature of certain plot elements.

Marie, played by Anne Parillaud, is a vampire living in modern Pittsburgh. Much like a female Dexter Morgan she has a moral code that requires her to kill only the criminals of society. After biting crime lord Salvatore 'The Shark' Macelli, played by Robert Loggia, she accidentally turns him into a vampire. It is up to Marie and undercover cop Gennaro, played by Anthony LaPaglia, to stop Macelli.

John Landis has a specific style to his "horror" movies that is felt in *Innocent Blood*. The violence and gore are undercut by jokes and visual humor that softens the blow of the horror. The mixture of genres makes the film entertaining to a wider variety of audience. While the casting of Parillaud is a strange choice of Marie, she is able to pull it off. Her accent is very strong and makes her a bit difficult to understand at times yet her movements and actions really solidify her as decent actress.

The story and concept is fun and the threat of seeing a mobster turn vampire and then turning his underlings into his vampire followers is a cool idea. Casting Don Rickles as a mob lawyer is fun to watch and creates some amusing scenes that make the movie as lighthearted as *An American Werewolf in London*. The effects in *Innocent Blood* are not as impressive as *An American Werewolf in London* but it still okay enough to keep people in the movie. Anthony LaPaglia is sort of the "dry white toast" of the movie. He does not really make a compelling character but he is the audience surrogate walking them through the movie.

Innocent Blood has a lot of elements of a movie made by a fan for fans. It is a vampire movie that takes a humorous look at the common tropes of the time and mocks it. Like a Joe Dante film, this movie is rife with cameos from Linnea Quigley, Sam Raimi, Tom Savini, Forrest J. Ackerman, Frank Oz, and Dario Argento which are amusing to see but occasionally take me out of the movie when saying "Hey, isn't that so and so?" during the film. Still, the love of the horror genre is felt and it does come off like a genuine appreciation towards films in a similar vein (pun not intended).

While not a very memorable movie, *Innocent Blood* is entertaining. The characters are not very well developed or unique enough to see them on a Buzzfeed list of awesome vampires. The movie is the perfect palate cleanser, it kills time and is entertaining but it works better as a movie you watch between thought provoking movies. As it is, *Innocent Blood* won't win any awards but it is at least well made and the character actors do an okay job taking two-dimensional characters some memorable features. Comparing this movie to the many other vampire movies out there I can say that the pace of *Innocent Blood* keeps the film moving. It does not waste time with filler or flashbacks to when Marie was human.

Innocent Blood is a fun movie that will entertain a variety of audiences. The effects are good and the humor is delightfully dark considering the horror that ensues. The acting is well done and the story is entertaining. The problem is that the movie is fairly forgettable when you consider the director's other works. There is nothing that really makes this movie stand out. The movie is clever, funny, and erotic. It feels like this is the sort of movie that would be ripe for a remake in the future.

It Follows

Modern horror often runs the risk of being stale and formulaic. *It Follows* is not only well-made but it is nightmarish to watch. It is not scary in the most typical sense. There are jump scares here and there but the fear comes from the lingering unease that is almost primal and set up artistically in this film.

College student Jay, played by Maika Monroe, goes on a date with a boy she has been seeing. After having sex, she is chloroformed and wakes up tied to a chair. Her date informs her that he has just passed a curse onto her. An entity will begin to follow her and will kill her if it comes into contact with her. She must have sex with someone else to pass along the curse or keep on the run from this entity.

This movie is beautifully shot. There are creative uses of panoramic lens and 360 degree shots that are astounding. The music is also really unnerving; it creates a sense of unease and dread throughout the entire movie. There are style choices in the costumes that make the movie feel retro and like a throwback to the 80s. At the same time there are futuristic fictional devices that don't exist currently that could imply that this is the near future.

The acting is incredibly believable. Maika Monroe shines as Jay. Her character transforms from a young woman in her sexual prime to one that is broken, terrified, and bordering insanity. *It Follows* is certainly a creepy movie but it is not the scariest movie of all time. It is a cerebral movie that will have you talking about it long after the final reel.

The Director/Writer has spoken about how the nature of this entity is more about being in a nightmare you can't escape. The nightmare aspect can easily be seen in the thematic elements that can easily be worked into the discussion. Things like: STDs, absentee parents, bad boy attraction etc. *It Follows* is certainly worth watching if you are into more cerebral thrills. Just don't expect a lot of answers to be given to you. You will need to interpret a lot for yourself. It feels like it took the basic idea of *Drag Me To Hell* and made it artistic, less gory, and less obvious.

Jupiter Ascending

Jupiter Ascending is a sci-fi movie directed by the Wachowskis that pays homage to a lot of the movies that came before it. There are elements of *Star Wars*, *Dune*, *Cloud Atlas*, and even *Brazil*. The cast is charismatic and a lot of fun to watch. It is a clever space opera that hopefully will get its audience despite the poor reviews.

Jupiter Jones, played by Mila Kunis, is a cleaning woman who hates her life. After going to sell her eggs at a fertility clinic, she is attacked by aliens. Caine Wise, played by Channing Tatum, saves her. Jupiter discovers that she is a member of the royal family, Abrasax, who control various planets and reduce the populations into a youth serum. Jupiter becomes entwined in assassination plots and power feuds.

Mila Kunis is cute as a button. She is a strong female protagonist that makes the story very relatable. Channing Tatum is good at playing a heroic space adventurer. Eddie Redmanye as Balem, the evil dynastic ruler, hams it up like a melodrama villain. Everyone is enjoyable in his or her part and make the movie entertaining.

The costumes are nothing short of amazing. The sets and the designs of this universe are unique and wildly fun. From the dinosaur guards to the ships that resemble Renaissance buildings, there was clearly a great deal of vision put into this movie. It was especially hilarious to see how even though the worlds are incredibly high tech they still have to deal with slow and inefficient bureaucrats. If you are a fan of sci-fi movies you will likely enjoy this movie. It is a smart movie that delivers on action with characters that really are enjoyable. It would be interesting to see if this grows into a series like the *Matrix* movies. It is certainly worth checking out for a good time at the movies.

Jurassic World

When I was in sixth grade I saw the first *Jurassic Park* movie and it amazed me. It was fun, it was scary, and it was smart. Two sequels later and things were not looking good for the *Jurassic Park* franchise. Unfortunately, it seems that the series has not aged well. While still being better than the past two sequels, *Jurassic World* leaves a lot to be desired.

Twenty-two years after the events of Isla Nublar, Jurassic World is a new and fully functioning theme park. Brothers Zach and Gray Mitchell take a trip to the park to visit their aunt Claire, the park's operations manager, played by Bryce Dallas Howard. Soon after their arrival one of the newest genetically created attractions, the Indominus Rex, escapes and starts a killing rampage. Owen Grady, played by Chris Pratt, is a Velociraptor trainer who comes to Claire's aid in stopping the rogue dinosaurs.

Jurassic World uses a distracting amount of C.G.I. Just about nothing looks real and at times it takes you out of the movie to be watching the equivalent of a cartoon. Even the door to the Jurassic World Park looked poorly pasted, like a Photoshop image. It made me nostalgic for the animatronics used in the original Jurassic Park film.

The acting is fine and Chris Pratt and Bryce Dallas Howard have a fun chemistry that works to make the movie entertaining. The problem is that the plot is juggling various balls and as an audience member I didn't know which one to focus on. Throughout the story you have the divorce plot of the parents of Zach and Gray, you have the escaped Indominus Rex, you have InGen hoping to use dinosaurs and military weapons, and you have a romance subplot with the two leads.

If producers come at us with a new *Jurassic Park* movie I hope that they at least have the originality to make a movie where they don't need kids in the cast. They borrow a lot of elements from the past movies, which they do seldom enough to not be obnoxious. There was some good build up to seeing what the Indominus Rex would look like. The problem was that the pay off was not worth it.

If ever there was a scene that showed me there was-- at one point-- a good movie idea here let me illustrate the following scene. Owen gets caught in an unexpected chain of events involving his velociraptors. He spies one in the grass and they both catch each other's eyes. There is a look of momentary understanding between the two of them before a rocket kills the raptor and sends Owen off his feet. Owen then stares silently at the burnt wreckage where his former friend used to stand. All of this is done without words and it is probably one of the best scenes in the movie.

Jurassic World is not a bad film but it is not a theater-worthy film either. I would recommend it for rental for sure. It is fun on occasion but lacks the story direction of any of the previous movies. There are moments that seem funny and self-aware but they are few and far between. If you are a fan of the rest of the franchise you will enjoy the beast on beast action and insane mad science on display. If you are looking to start the franchise I recommend going back to the beginning before seeing this one.

Krampus

Movies like *Rare Exports* and *Gremlins* hold a place in our hearts as they take the clichés and tropes of holiday movies and add dark elements to make it original. Krampus falls into this category. From the director of *Trick 'r Treat*, *Krampus* creates a fun and horrific tale that is sure to become a Christmas classic for horror fans.

Krampus takes place on a Christmas Eve in a suburban household where a family has gotten together to celebrate. The family is at each other's throats and the mood becomes dour as Max, the young son of the household, writes a letter to Santa that gets mocked mercilessly by the rest of the family. Max tears up the letter and it magically summons the Krampus, a monstrous spirit of Christmas that punishes bad behavior rather than rewarding the good, like Santa Claus.

The movie has a great use of practical effects mixed with some CGI. The elements of horror are there and they are quite effective. Dolls normally are not scary to me, however the creatures developed for this film are something out of nightmares. Even the look of the Krampus is dreadful to behold. The story is dark and the elements of humor contrast well to make it something really memorable.

The acting is fun and the movie is enjoyable. If there is one thing that could be improved it would be to make this movie a hard R rating rather than PG-13. The movie has elements of terror but there are a few moments that feel like they are holding back their punches for the lesser ratings. This minor detail is the only thing holding back this great movie.

Krampus will grow to become a new holiday classic. It is well made and the story is a lot of fun. It will be sure to entertain anyone that is a fan of dark subjects or horror. The cast plays it very seriously despite the silly material. It is a different movie that is sure to entertain with its griping characters and insane creatures.

Last Shift

When it comes to movies, something under the radar can often be an unexpected surprise. Such is the case with *Last Shift*. The movie shows a great eye for the disturbing and uses its lonesome setting at a closing police station as a creepy backdrop for a dark "bottle" movie.

Rookie police officer Jessica Loren, played by Juliana Harkavy, has the last shift at a closing police station. Left alone, she begins seeing and hearing eerie things that suggest the supernatural. As events get more and more disturbing she finds that it has something to do with the Charles Manson-style cult, which was brought in a year prior.

The movie has a great eye for the disturbing. The imagery of the ghosts, and the way they show the hauntings is something that will linger with you long after the movie has ended. *Last Shift* builds on its characters and creates a disturbing sense of tension that builds until the twisted end.

The acting is solid and the character of Jessica is likable, adding to the tragedy of the events that befall her. I recommend this movie for anyone who is looking for horror tale that is truly haunting and disturbing. It will linger in your thoughts and keep you wondering what was real and what was illusionary. The jump-scares are effective and put to good use which is rare for the genre. *Last Shift* shows a quality seldom seen in horror films.

Lazarus Effect
If you were too scared or interested in *Pet Sematary* or the film *The Re-Animator* this movie would be right up your alley. The acting is good but isn't enough to save an otherwise dull movie that is heavy on jump scares and light on story. The effects are laughable and the death scenes are forgettable.

A group of medical scientists led by Frank, played by Mark Duplass, and Zoe, played by Olivia Wilde, are attempting to bring animals back to life using a serum called Lazarus. Zoe accidentally dies in a lab experiment so Frank and his team inject her with the serum bringing her back to life. Soon she is showing all sorts of signs of new psychic powers.

Let's start with the fact that much like *Lucy* this movie spreads the myth that humans only use 10% of their brains at a time. When injected with the serum creatures all of a sudden have access to all their brain and are psychic powerhouses. There is very little time developing the characters and even less showing us how Zoe goes from good to evil. She just flips her evil switch and then starts a kill spree.

The best aspect of this movie is that the actors are great at their roles. They are entertaining and charming, for the most part. The problem is that they are not given good material to work with. Even the best carpenter can't make a great house if he is supplied with only balsa wood. The death scenes seem lazy and not scary in the slightest. There are four deaths in total and two of them are necks breaking.

The movie is too boring to be scary. This is the sort of movie that makes me never want to go see a PG-13 horror movie. It might be passable as an HBO movie that you catch during a channel surfing session. It is disappointing that such a trite movie got green lit in the first place. As Jud Crandall said in *Pet Sematary* "Sometimes dead is better."

Lullaby

Lullaby is a chore to watch. The characters are all terribly unlikeable people. The story is ludicrous and the unpleasant material in the movie is matched only by acting that is on par with DMV employees. The predictability of this plot becomes evident really soon into the film, which is disappointing.

John is a young man caring for a young girl and baby. While taking care of these kids at a nice suburban home, it becomes evident that John is not actually their parent. Their actual parents have been injured and are being kept in the basement. John has an insane fascination with the mother of this family and his history with her has led to him invading their home.

The beginning of the film prior to discovering John's nature is very odd to watch. The acting is on par with imagining aliens coming to Earth and pretending to be casual humans in human skin and yet not being natural in any delivery. John seems bored then uncomfortable. The "twist" is predictable and while it is supposed to be disturbing it mostly comes off as cheap. I've seen more natural deliveries from C3P0 than some of the actors on screen.

The biggest movie plot hole is that the police have the house surrounded and John constantly walks around the windows. The police snipers or a semi-competent S.W.A.T. team would have ended this movie a long time ago. We would not have to deal with the terrible relationship drama of the married couple in the basement and the insanity of John. There are scenes where the baby that John is watching is crying and the baby is obviously very visibly upset. It makes the movie come off really unpleasant and I feel very disappointed that they made a baby sad for this movie. It simply is not worth it.

If there is a redeeming factor to _Lullaby_ it is that there are scenes that are made to make you feel uncomfortable that are successful at their purpose. At one point a neighbor visits John while he is with the kids and she wanders into the house uninvited, stands incredibly close to John, and even eats some of his food. It is an invasive scene but the mood is achieved.

If they could re-write this movie I can think of a few items that would polish it up. For one thing, seeing the actual home invasion in a flashback would have worked. It would have added some tension to the movie. There is also a scene where the little girl has diabetes and passes out.

While discussing the option of releasing the mother to give the girl her insulin the next scene just shows John giving the now conscious girl a glass of water. That disconnect really could have had a transition that made what occurred much more clear. Then, when it is revealed that John is violent it gets disturbing fast. When on the phone to police negotiators he basically says he will rape and gut the kids if the police do not turn back on the electricity. Now whether or not the character would actually do that is up for debate but it still makes the central character of the narrative pretty despicable to even seriously suggest that to the police.

Lullaby is not an entertaining movie. The characters are wildly unlikable and since the writing direction comes off more like a poor stage play than a film there is very little to keep a person interested. This is the sort of movie that might have worked back in the early 90s when twists in movies were all the rage and nobody had smartphones to contend with for the attention of the viewer. Also with so many better movies, even in the independent arena there are a lot of reasons to make sure that the product is decent. If you are looking for a movie about home invasions that have some brains I suggest *Panic Room, When a Stranger Calls,* or the most recent version of *Mother's Day.*

Mad Max: Fury Road

The *Mad Max* franchise is one of high-octane action and *Fury Road* is no exception. After a brief narration the movie takes ahold of your adrenal gland and bites down hard. The action is nearly non-stop, the acting is solid, and the effects are very bombastic and fun.

"Mad" Max Rockatansky, played by Tom Hardy, roams the wasteland of post-nuclear war Australia. He is captured by a strange gang called the War Boys and used as a blood bag for Nux, a War Boy played by Nicholas Hoult. After a daring escape he finds that the War Boys leader had wives that escaped with Furiosa, played by Charlize Theron. Max decides to help out the wives in escaping their tyrannical matrimony.

The acting is fantastic. Charlize Theron is a believable action star. Nicholas Hoult brings a great performance as a zealous character that is strengthened by war like an ancient Viking. The effects are insane and are as bombastic as a Baz Luhrmann movie. There are flame throwers everywhere, people on stilts, and people that use bungee cords.

The story itself is much like a western. Max could be considered the Clint Eastwood "Man with no name." The only big flaw is that not much is explained. Why is Furiosa missing an arm? Who is the girl Max always sees in hallucinations? Still, the movie doesn't seem weakened by not giving definitive answers. It is beautifully filmed and doesn't let up on the action scenes. If you are a fan of the franchise or action films in general it is a must see. It is stylistic and fun. You don't need to be familiar with the original material.

Moose: The Movie

Making a movie is a hard and expensive process that takes long hours and loads of teamwork. It is impressive to see local Alaskans work so hard to make a project that is better than most Syfy channel movies. The Carpenter brothers have made independent films before but not one so "community minded." *Moose: The Movie* has the help of many folks from throughout Wasilla and has created a unique fictional town that could rival Mayberry or Green Acres for colorful characters.

Moose: The Movie begins with the native tale of a Moosetaur (a half-man and half-moose) that is banished to the underworld. When two campers disturb the totem pole, which acts as a seal to the underworld, the Moosetaur returns to the small Alaskan town of Gangrene Gulch and begins a killing spree. It's up to the local deputy and a coroner's assistant to solve the murders and dispatch with the ancient evil.

The movie is beautifully shot and has some great nature photography. The cast gives you their best and they are clearly able to express themselves comically. The writing is fun and has a charm that that crackles with sparks of wit. The colorful characters make it an entertaining movie and the tight editing gives it almost cartoonish timing.

My only complaints are fairly minor nitpicky reviewer stuff like small continuity errors. Since this is an extremely low budget movie it is free from a lot of that criticism. They get what they can work with, and the end product is nothing to be ashamed of. If there were one minor thing I would change it would be to remove at least one of the two pairs of bumbling comic relief.

Alaska, this is YOUR movie. Enjoy it. The locals are having fun, the humor is not malicious, and it is clearly a labor of love. If you are from Alaska you should definitely see this movie if you can. If you aren't from Alaska you should still see it for some good humor and to see that even on a low budget a good movie can be made.

Morgan

Morgan is a science fiction movie that disappoints on several levels. The trailer made the Morgan character appear to have telekinetic powers. This turned out to just be clever editing. The cast if full of really talented and well-known actors and the shots are often very pretty. The writing makes the scientists out to be morons and the plot twist is telegraphed and stupid.

After a genetically created child, Morgan, played by Anya Taylor-Joy, has a tantrum and stabs a doctor in the eye, the company funding the experiment sends a risk manager to determine the viability of the experiment. As it turns out Morgan is a highly developed weapon that knows all sorts of deadly martial arts. She soon overtakes her captors and escapes. It is up to the risk manager to determine how to proceed.

The characters are performed well but are poorly written and developed. The scientists created a human out of artificial DNA, so the question as to her personal rights could have been explored, but instead it is forgotten. They have become emotionally attached to Morgan so that complicates matters greatly. The scientists also have no methods of tracking her whereabouts despite the fact they let Morgan go outside often.

They also have no contingency if Morgan attacks them. The scientists are awful at their jobs. Even the scientists in

Jurassic Park had the lysine contingency just in case. It is vaguely implied that one of the scientists has a lesbian attraction to Morgan. That is not explored either though. To this film's credit there are some great nature shots. It is a pretty movie, at the very least.

Morgan is a movie that squanders good actors in a movie that is subpar at best. The characters are poorly developed and the story is ridiculous. The best thing about this dull movie is that the running time is short. It is a disappointing film that even talented actors cannot save. The twist does not help this movie. Since it fails to entertain it is very difficult to recommend this forgettable movie.

Narcopolis

Narcopolis is a neo-noir science fiction thriller. The movie quality is good, the acting is so-so, but the story itself is a convoluted mess. Just when you think you might understand what is happening in this story it takes a bizarre turn and leaves you wondering why the filmmakers decided to proceed to take the story in such a strange way.

Narcopolis takes place in the distant future of 2024 where in 2019 drugs have become legalized across the board. Pharmaceutical corporations sell the drugs and special cops called Drecks are created to arrest the drug dealers who still trade in the black market. After finding a mysterious body the Dreck, Frank Grieves finds out that legalization comes at a price.

On paper this sounds like a modern version of *Reefer Madness*. It has away more in common with another neo-noir film, *Blade Runner.* The similarities are abundant:

- Blade Runner takes place in 2019, this movie has major plot elements that begin in 2019.
- Both films feature a cop that has a title that is a slang term (Blade Runner/Dreck).
- Both officers basically work for the corporations to remove problems that the corporations are responsible for causing.
- Both officers have futuristic weapons that are fairly similar.

At times I longed for the futuristic ads welcoming a new life in the off-world colonies because despite the similarities to *Blade Runner,* this film does not bring any of the brains to the table that *Blade Runner* did.

At about the halfway point of the film the story introduces time travel through drug use. Time travel movies are somewhat tricky as it is and often require a lot of exposition to truly get the audience onboard. Adding it like a last-minute thought is a really bad idea that just makes the movie confusing. As if that was not bad enough the time travel idea makes the ending a paradox that should loop itself through eternity.

The bummer about this film is that the central idea is not a bad one. Making a dystopian movie about a world where all drugs are legal could have been interesting and smart. The political and societal implications could have been intriguing and really built a world that is terrifying no matter what your views on legalization are. Instead it felt like the writer just wanted to make a movie that people would find bizarre. The effects are not terrible but that alone does not make a movie good.

The cast does an okay job given the material. The only person that stands out is Jonathan Pryce. He has a part that is so small that it feels like the producers wasted an opportunity with him. There isn't anyone who sticks out and the performances are wholly forgettable. If only somebody brought a unique performance or some nuance to this film it might have elevated the quality of the film quite a bit.

The noir setting of London is not bad. There are elements of dark cynicism and moral ambiguity that is par for the course with noir. To add to the confusion the movie begins in the year 2044 then leaps to 2024, and then back again. I am sure that if I had multiple viewings I might understand it a little better. The problem is that the characters are not compelling enough to want to view it multiple times. The ending is bizarre and the build up to it seems like the setup to a lame punch line that causes nobody to laugh.

When it comes to recommending *Narcopolis*, I would say this movie is a dud. The characters are not people you want to go on the journey with and the story is a mess of sci-fi themes that might as well have been created from magnetic poetry on a refrigerator. Even the people that enjoy bad movies might find it a bit tedious. Save your time and watch *Blade Runner*.

Operation Avalanche

Operation Avalanche is a clever movie that takes the moon landing conspiracy theory and weaves an entertaining story out of the concept. The story is fascinating, the characters show depth, and the film style is surprisingly authentic looking. The soundtrack is also very fun and captures the time period well.

Operation Avalanche is a found footage mockumentary about two CIA agents that are working to find a KGB mole working in NASA during the space race to the moon. During their investigation they discover that NASA will never be able to successfully achieve the lunar mission. Using special effects methods learned from Stanley Kubrick, the agents then attempt to go about faking a moon landing to fool the public that NASA has done the impossible.

The footage of *Operation Avalanche* has a very authentic look. The film has an old quality with minor scratches and imperfections that film stock regularly had. The costumes, sets, and even a car chase all have a sense of authenticity to them. This realism adds to the tension of the thrills, which ensue in the conspiracy plot in the film. Their skills of the writing and acting was very noteworthy and the script was very taut, witty, and smart.

If you are interested in a film that does something completely different, give *Operation Avalanche* a try. The mixture of genres and smart ideas come together to remind audiences what movies can do as an art form. They should occasionally challenge our perceptions and our ideas and still entertain. *Operation Avalanche* remarkably manages to achieve this lofty goal.

Open Water

Open Water is a 2003 horror movie shot on a shoe-string

budget about the true story of Tom and Eileen Lonergan, a vacationing couple that went scuba diving in 1998 in the Bahamas and were left out in open sea. The movie portrays what folks suppose happened to them using actors that are fairly unknown, with the exception of Steve Lemme of Broken Lizard that plays an uncredited diver. The camera filters used give the movie an incredibly cheap feel.

Daniel Kintner, played by Daniel Travis, and Susan Watkins, played by Blanchard Ryan, are a young couple that are having some relationship difficulties. They decide to go scuba diving together and join a group on a on an ocean boat. While on the boat a head count is taken and they mistakenly count 20 instead of the 18 that are there. Daniel and Susan have been left behind in the ocean and the boat is nowhere to be found.

Open Water capitalizes on the uneasy feeling one might get swimming alone in the ocean. There is very little action and considering that the couple finds themselves attacked by both jellyfish and sharks, there is very little actually seen on screen. The sound quality is fairly poor and the film looks like a home video. Why the filmmakers decided upon this is a bit baffling. The dialogue is forgettable and there are not a lot of compelling reasons to captivate the viewer. The thing that this movie has going for it is that it has a creepy premise that is based on a terrible true story. The problem is that it is really not something that needed to be told in the length of a feature length film. This story could probably have a just been a half hour documentary that would have been more interesting.

The Netflix sleeve claimed that *Open Water* is a mix of *Jaws* and *the Blair Witch Project*. I think that is a bit of a stretch.

For one thing, the sharks are more like an unfortunate by-product of being the ocean where in *Jaws* the shark is the antagonist of the film. It is also not like The Blair Witch Project since the camera operator does not play a part directly in the film. The movie is creepy as an idea but fails to be scary. There are a lot more movies that are "based on a true story" that involve a lot more drama, are much more horrific, and have characters that are more developed. If you are looking in the horror genre check into *Wolf Creek* or the original *Texas Chainsaw Massacre* and if you are looking into drama on the high seas look no further than *The Perfect Storm*.

I'll admit the ocean can be eerie. When I imagine swimming in open water it gives me the sort of tingly fear that I'd feel if I were floating in space. Except in the ocean, there could be giants living in the dark lurking and possibly hunting you. For all the build up, the tragedy is somewhat underwhelming by the lack of character development and the shoddy quality of the film and sound.

Is *Open Water* worth seeing? Probably not, considering that there have been movies that have attempted what this film has done and succeeded. *Open Water* is the sort of movie that you watch and quickly forget because nothing stands out. Instead you might go into the ocean and if you swim in the open ocean you might feel a chill as you slowly recollect the basic plot of this movie. *Open Water* has become the campfire story that people will end up telling kids about traveling and what terrifying things can occur to a person when their guard is not kept up.

Paranormal Activity: The Ghost Dimension

For as long as there have been Paranormal Activity movies I have been an avid watcher. I defended each movie thinking that there was some method to the madness and that one movie would reveal the answers to all the questions I had. I am a fool. *Paranormal Activity: The Ghost Dimension* touts itself as the sixth and final installment, which is supposed to tie all the loose ends. Instead, this movie is a testament how lazy filmmakers are and how gullible they view their audiences.

Starting off with the final events of Paranormal Activity 3, the ending is re-capped. Then we are taken 25 years later to find that a new family has moved into the house. They discover an old video camera and a box of old VHS videos. The videos are of Katie and Kristi doing ritualistic cult stuff while the camera is discovered to have the ability to see the demon Tobi. They attempt to put an end to the demon's hold on their house and hopefully rid their family of the curse that is now afflicting them.

If this movie was not a Paranormal Activity movie the spirit camera idea might have worked. As it is, it comes off as really stupid and takes all the fear away when you see Tobi as an entity and even more so when you see he has a face. There is nothing wholly remarkable about this movie and really it answers no big burning questions you might have had if you are a fan of the franchise. If anything it raises more questions and even creates an ending that would be suitable for a sequel that nobody will be asking for.

What made the Paranormal Activity movies so great were the sense of dread and powerlessness that was created in something that you could not see. It was left up largely to the imagination to develop why it was doing what it was. As the mythos grew the quality of the narrative dipped with each foray into suburban horror.

So why was this made? To put it simply, the Paranormal Activity movies are lessons in making movies on the cheap. They have a built-in audience and they cost very little to make. For a rough $10 million dollar budget they have made out well, raking in nearly $80 million dollars. This movie is such an obvious cash-grab that I am shocked they didn't split it into two parts. None of the former cast that you have come to enjoy is there and the ending is awful. Even if you are a die-hard fan of the franchise don't bother, there are much better movies out there.

REC 4: Apocalypse

REC 4: Apocalypse follows the events that occurred at the end of the second film. Considered the final film of the franchise, *REC 4* tries to wrap up the story of Angela Vidal. The acting is decent and the effects are gory and fun. The setting of a huge, old boat is a great change because, like most bottle movies, it creates a sense of claustrophobia and unease.

Angela Vidal, played by Manuela Velasco, is found in the apartment building that was quarantined in the first two films. A few soldiers rescue her before the building is blown up. She wakes up in a lab onboard a large boat. She and the soldiers that saved her are trying to find out what occurred and make sure that the sickness doesn't spread any further.

There are several references to the previous films, which is great for fans of the series. An old woman from the wedding in the third film is staying aboard the boat as well. As for how this expands the entire *REC* storyline, it felt like it created more questions than answers. For example, the first movie showed that the disease was found as the source for demonic possession. The second establishes that these creatures can be attacked by holy symbols. The third showed how the infected had reflections that were demonic. This film talks about how the disease is a parasite but that is about it.

The acting is good and the action is a lot of fun. It is not often you can watch a guy killing groups of rage zombies and monkeys with a boat motor. It is a silly movie but it is also fun. It at least brings back the character of Angela so we can see what became of her and what her fate inevitably will be. If they didn't say this was the final movie I think it would have easily found a way to build up a sequel using other actors.

REC 4: Apocalypse is a good movie. I would recommend it to any horror fan but only if you have seen the past films. I think they are some of the most consistently good zombie movies out there. If you are in the mood for a series that is foreign and takes chances, give the *REC* series a try. They are sure to entertain.

Rogue One: A Star Wars Story

Rogue One: A Star Wars Story is a standalone film in the Star Wars cinematic universe. The special effects are great, showing the audience the universe at the dawn of the rebellion. The performances are good and showcase the skilled actors in a variety of complex roles. If there was a flaw to this movie, it is that this tale takes the longest route to a get to the crux of the story.

Rogue One centers on the character, Jyn Erso, played by Felicity Jones. She is the daughter of Galen Erso who is the designer of the Death Star. After falling into the hands of the rebels, Jyn must locate her father. She meets up with an eclectic group of fighters and together they go on a mission to get the Death Star plans in the hope of finding a flaw that might be a glimmer of hope for the rebellion.

The story is dark and foreboding, fitting right in with the mood of *The Empire Strikes Back*. The plot meanders a bit and some scenes feel like they could have been left on the cutting room floor. There are also strange choices such as the choice not to do a text crawl in the beginning of the film. Since Star Wars has always paid homage to old serial films, like Flash Gordon, it seems like a move to change that vision. There was also the odd choice to bring General Tarkin, who was played by the deceased Peter Cushing, back in CGI form. This was not the only character change as the film includes a young Princess Leia who was also given the CGI treatment. While they look good for CGI doubles and the actors play the part well, it looks a bit odd and the effect took me out of the movie.

Felicity Jones plays a great lead and the rest of the cast show a level of skill needed to make the scenes have the depth needed for a darker Star Wars film. It was fun to see Darth Vader again on screen and hear the voice by James Earl Jones in all its glory. The special effects are solid and exciting but sometimes have the look of a video game cut scene. This was especially evident during the space battles. The robot character K-2SO, voiced by Alan Tudyk, often steals the scene with his wry humor.

I recommend this movie for Star Wars fans. For others who might be new to the franchise it might be a bit confusing. The theme of heroism and sacrifice during war is still relevant and takes a unique approach to the subject of the horrors of war and hope. It takes the universe that many of us enjoy and looks at it from a different angle, which may or may not be compelling depending solely on your point of view. As Obi Wan once said, "Luke, you're going to find that many of the truths we cling to depend greatly on our own point of view."

R.O.T.O.R

R.O.T.O.R is a science fiction movie that seems to rely on the ideas of movies that came before it. It is one part *Robocop* and one part *Terminator* and only entertaining to those people who are into movies that are "so bad they are good." Even the poster is a blatant rip-off of *Mad Max*. R.O.T.O.R is basically banking on the fame of other movies to make people watch it.

Barrett Coldyron has created a robotic police officer. They call the new mechanical officer R.O.T.O.R., which stands for Robotic Officer Tactical Operation Research. During some tests a mistake occurs that causes R.O.T.O.R to become active. When it does it is programmed to judge and execute. It finds a couple speeding on the road and kills the male driver. The female passenger goes on the run with the killer robot hot on her trail.

The movie has some amusing dialogue. Most of it is southern slang that would make Huckleberry Hound feel right at home. There is a wisecracking robot sidekick for the scientist who is stupid but it is sort of fun when you pretend that this is the same company that sold Rocky Balboa the robot that he gave to Pauly in *Rocky IV*. There is also an unexpected ending, which was appreciated given the unoriginal turd that the audience is subjected to.

The acting is pretty bad. The characters just do not have the gravitas to make you believe the words coming out of their mouths. They should have realized this movie was a turkey from day one and decided instead to perform it as melodramatically as possible. This gives nothing memorable and I am pretty sure this was a lot of the actor's first and last movie to perform in.

The story is ridiculous. It is never explained how R.O.T.O.R has a human outer shell. There is no explanation for its weaknesses and its weaknesses are truly bizarre. For instance, car horns are too loud for it. R.O.T.O.R also expresses frustration regularly, which makes no sense for a robot. In fact, there is little that does make sense. Let us imagine that crime was so bad that police needed robotic help. Why would they make one that is programmed like Judge Dredd? We would still have rights. I am pretty sure that the writers of this film have no clue how a computer works, much less how a robot would function. You cannot just have a robot switch on and go on a killing spree. The creator must have made it to kill or there is a huge glitch. So either the creator is incompetent or just evil.

The style of the film is bizarre. There are nameplates that are the same height as doorknobs, all establishing shots have the day and time labeled on them as if they matter and the end of the film does not match with what we saw at the beginning in flashback. Most of the movie is told in flashback and it makes me wonder how boring it must have been for the person listening to Coldyron tell every minute detail of his life in this story, "I woke up, had some orange juice and my vitamins, then I went roping stumps." Riveting. There is also the addition of the female character, Steele, who is there simply to fight the robot in a skunk colored mullet.

R.O.T.O.R is a movie for a very select audience and unfortunately I was not included. The acting is not worth mentioning and the story is nothing new. If you are looking for robot movies with some meat on the bones look no further than *Robocop* and the *Terminator*. If you are looking for something more recent try *Ex Machina*. This movie is not exciting and holds no thrills. It is a clear cash grab attempting to cash-in on the popular movies of the decade. It is essentially a *Mac and Me* without the obvious product placements.

San Andreas

This movie is not good and I honestly don't expect to remember it for long. It is a cookie-cutter disaster film that is predictable and void of originality. Even if you can suspend your disbelief enough to enjoy the action, it is ruined by bad C.G.I. of which would be more appropriate for a cut-scene in a video game. It should have been a lot more fun considering the cast.

Los Angeles Fire Department helicopter rescue pilot Ray Gaines, played by Dwayne "The Rock" Johnson, is in the midst of a divorce from his wife Emma, played Carla

Gugino. After discovering that Emma and his daughter Blake, played by Alexandra Daddario, are moving in with Emma's new boyfriend, Ray is noticeably upset. Soon a series of earthquakes tear the city apart and it's up to Ray to save his estranged family.

I was irritated that Ray is supposed to be a heroic fireman when the first thing he does in a massive crisis is basically steal a helicopter and use it to rescue his own family. People are dying left and right of him and you can count on half a hand the amount of times he goes out of his way to save strangers. Besides the rotten protagonist we have the massive dose of 9-11 and Titanic imagery that seems more like pandering than homage.

The C.G.I does no favors for this movie. Most of the shots look like green screen nightmares or the shots of people who move with the same realism of a living ventriloquist dummy. The plot is just what you'd expect from a disaster movie and is incredibly predictable. Some of the scenes even felt added for filler material to make it full length.

The writing is so weak that at no point did I feel that the main characters were at risk. With nothing at risk it really doesn't make me give a crap what the characters do since the movie doesn't have the guts to do something risky or original. In the end we get a movie that gives us a weak visual spectacle of an earthquake as seen by folks that, by all rights, should be dead several times over.

If they went for a more aware, tongue-in-cheek disaster movie this might have been great. The Rock and the rest of the cast would have been able to accomplish that. As it is I wouldn't recommend this movie unless you are a die-hard fan of the Rock or just have a desire for bad science and patriotic imagery. It might be worth a rental if it wasn't so forgettable.

Sgt. Kabukiman N.Y.P.D.

Sgt. Kabukiman N.Y.P.D is a superhero comedy film from Troma, which is as over-the-top and exploitative as any of their other productions. The movie is funny and entertaining and the action is slapstick and visually hilarious. *Sgt. Kabukiman N.Y.P.D* is an unexpected gem that needs to be seen.

Detective Harry Griswold, played by Rick Gianasi, is in the audience of a Kaubuki version of the Odd Couple when a shoot-out kills the actors. In his last breath one of the actors grants Griswold the powers of Kabukiman. A mystical superhero with the power of flight and uses Japanese themed weaponry such as chopsticks and sushi. He is summoned by Lotus, the alluring granddaughter of the Kabuki actor who gave Harry his new powers. Together they train him to overcome an entity known as "The Evil One."

This movie is akin to watching a detective movie with cartoonish effects, sounds and insane over-the-top scenes of violence and sex. The actors do a great job playing it straight and taking the insane material and making it work. For example in the first scene we see yuppies doing coke off a new Mercedes Benz while a killer in a wig murders a family. The dialogue is silly and full of one-liners but the there is a lot of straight performances that give it the gravitas needed.

If there was anything that needs to be improved it is the production value. The sound often has an echo and the film itself looks more like it was made in the 70s instead of the 90s. The campy quality is still fantastic to watch. They even have their own scene transition effect that is reminiscent of the sixties Batman television show. The effects are cheesy but that makes it more of a joy to watch since it almost comes off as something a bunch of friends made after drinking lots of Mountain Dew and watching late night cable television.

If you come into this movie wanting a serious movie then you are going to be disappointed. Like most Troma movies, your enjoyment of their movies depends on your ability to check your mind at the door. The movie is cinematic cotton candy. You know it is not good for you but it tastes fantastic, so you take your chances. There are ridiculous scenes of violence that gives *Sgt. Kabukiman N.Y.P.D* its own unique style. For example: Kabukiman sees a hooker with her pimp so he wraps them up and cuts them into sushi or he magically turns a villain into hot dogs because he is constantly called a "weinie" by his fellow criminals.

Sgt. Kabukiman N.Y.P.D is the sort of film that my high school self would have loved. It has zany dialogue, insane cartoonish action, and bare breasted women. As an adult it has just the comic humor still entertains me with its quick wit and bizarre gross-out effects. The main villain's plan is a bit ambiguous until the very end when he turns into a Lovecraftian beast called The Evil One. Like the Naked Gun films this movie has many moments of hilarity that rely on site gags. These include comedy gold like the hard boiled detective walking into his apartment which is covered in piles of empty beer cans.

Sgt. Kabukiman N.Y.P.D is a fun distraction that would find itself on any film fan's shelf. It holds no great wisdom or truth, but it does not claim to either. In my opinion it is even better than *The Toxic Avenger* but still not to the quality of *Cannibal! The Musical.* There are loads of Troma movies available for free now online and this is certainly one worth checking out. If you are not familiar at all with Troma or you are a fan of the Troma style, you should certainly give this movie a chance. You will likely not be disappointed.

Sinister 2

Sinister 2 is the sequel to the supernatural horror film Sinister. The film follows the character of Deputy So & So as he tries to save a family from the curse of Bughuul. The acting is good and the story is interesting. It might not be as compelling as the original but it is entertaining in its own right with characters that are interesting and a story that is captivating.

After the death of the Oswalt family Ex Deputy So & So has become a private investigator. He spends his free time investigating the Bughuul curse and attempting to stop it in its tracks by burning the houses down. He meets Courtney Collins, played by Shannyn Sossamon, at an old home with her two sons. Ex Deputy So & So then goes out of his way to attempt to protect the family from the demon. Meanwhile, her abusive estranged husband torments Courtney and her family.

The cast does a decent job at being charming and likable. The entire time you really do not want anything bad to happen to them. The only exception is the abusive father of the family, which is so cartoonish and over-the-top that he might as well have had hooves for feet and horns on his head. Shannyn Shossamon and the Ex Deputy have a cute chemistry that seems to really work for the story.

The story is pretty entertaining. We get a mix of a point of views from the Ex Deputy, a character from the first film that is likable and has a reason for continuing his journey, as well as the point of view of the one of the kids, Dylan, as Bughuul and his cadre of evil children try to corrupt him. The kills in this movie are much more brutal than in the previous film and get a lot more extreme at times. For example their one kill involves nailing adults to the floor and having rats burrow through their stomachs so the victims bleed to death. All the while he is filming this with a Super 8 camera. I do think that the Ex Deputy probably should have been a lot more damaged psychologically after the things he has seen and the supernatural events he has faced. Still, he portrays the fact that he is afraid and he seems to know that he is in over his head.

The imagery is very dark and eerie. The filter that was chosen gives the screen an almost constant sense of gritty darkness. The Super 8 films are still creepy to watch but have taken on a more haunting air since the audience is watching the children watch the videos and slowly become possessed by the powers of the evil demonic force. The Bughuul legend is not expanded upon nearly as much as I would have personally liked. It is basically a "boogie man" that has always existed and is present all over the world throughout history.

The writers have created characters that are clearly "okay to kill" because they are despicable. It makes me wonder if they are making up for murdering the entire family in the last film. The comeuppance kills are earned, but it makes it more of an act of karma instead of horror and it kind of takes away from the overall mood of the film. I am not sure what else they can do with this story so I hope that the producers do not decide to continue to milk this franchise.

Sinister 2 is worth seeing if you were a fan of the first movie. It is a smart follow-up that seems to care about creating a story that is very creepy. It does have a much more positive ending as well so it feels like evil has not won by the conclusion. If you are not familiar with the events of the first film it will be a bit difficult to follow so I recommend watching this immediately after to get a feeling that the continuity of the story is unbroken.

Sonny Boy

If you are a looking for a movie that is one part *The Cabinet of Dr. Caligari* and another part *Unleashed*, I would still suggest you try a different movie because *Sonny Boy* is off the rails. This movie is unpleasant and is not made well enough to warrant any one searching it out other than hipsters looking for something to watch ironically. It is exploitative, predictable, and it feels like a joke on the audience.

A criminal named Weasel, played by Brad Dourif, robs and kills a young couple. When he goes to fence the stolen items, he finds a baby in the backseat. The redneck couple that fence the material decide to take the baby. They name the baby Sonny Boy and raise him like an animal. The family cuts off his tongue and train him to kill their enemies and eat them.

As I mentioned, this movie is unpleasant. A child getting his tongue cut out and being drug behind a car is not something I ever need to imagine. Meanwhile, the baby playing Sonny Boy is crying constantly like he is miserable being on screen. Whatever it took to make that baby upset was not worth it. The redneck family is insane. The man, Slue, is a hulk that gets mad constantly, kicks a pig when it is in his way and slaps anyone who crosses him. The woman, Pearl, is played by a cross-dressing David Carradine.

The movie quality is very poor. The screen looks so scratchy that it appears to be edited in a rock tumbler. Between scene transitions, a form of dueling banjos play as if to make the audience feel like at anytime the characters will be raped by hillbillies. Not that there are not a few charms to this movie. Brad Dourif could read the phone book and be awesome. He tries to be memorable every time he is on screen. Paul L. Smith does a great job as Slue. I used to think he was only memorable for being in *Pieces* but he really is great as acting like an abusive butt-head in this film.

The last fifteen minutes has all the real action in the movie. It feels like the bulk of the budget went to the shoot-out scene, which was covered in explosions and fireballs. The problem is that this movie is nothing new. It is a plot about a man who takes a pitiable man/creature and makes him into his killing tool. When people figure out there is a killer amok they gather a mob and go after them. They did not even make a story that seemed to flow logically. At one point Sonny Boy is being attacked by an angry mob and then the screen just says "Three days later." We suddenly see Sonny Boy hanging out in the desert and he apparently has a girlfriend.

Who decided to put David Carradine in a dress and have him play a woman? It is so strange and then he also wrote and performed the intro song in the film. It is distracting and it does not add anything to the movie. There is a lot of filler in the movie in the attempt to make Sonny Boy seem more vulnerable. Things like having him leer at a couple he comes across having sex in an abandoned house. It does not make him seem like a tragic character but more of a creep.

There few things that this movie has going for it do not make it worth seeing. I guess if you are a fan of the bizarre or you might be a fan of obscure Yugoslavian actress Savina Gersak then it might be worth your time. Otherwise, you can see most of these actors doing much better movies. It is amazing that a movie like this ever was green lighted. If it was funnier I could excuse the weirdness but it was devoid of humor and instead seemed to feed of the confusion of the audience.

Spectre

Skyfall left the bar fairly high for the last James Bond movie. *Spectre* is the first of the Daniel Craig series of Bond movies, which feels like a return to the ridiculous plot holes and unrealistic situations that the James Bond films were famous for. It comes off more like a colossal step back instead of an advance in character.

James Bond, played by Daniel Craig, receives a message

from the late M, played by Dame Judi Dench. She tells James to find and kill a man who leads to a conspiracy that all the villains of his past had been tied to a secret organization led by one evil man. The organization is Spectre and the evil man is Ernst Stavro Blofeld, played by Christoph Waltz.

Spectre is not lacking in atmosphere. There are some beautiful shots of Mexico City during a day of the dead celebration complete with amazing skull costumes. The acting is okay and folks seem like they are having fun with their roles. However, the rest of the film cruises into the depths of disappointment.

The casting of Monica Belluci and Dave Bautista is a mystery since their parts are miniscule and both are more talented then the parts they were given. There are huge plot holes, which took me out of the movie. Even for a James Bond movie, I should not be puzzled by events on screen. For example, how is an evil organization secret if they give jewelry to the members that displays their membership?

Lea Seydoux does a fine job as the love interest and seems capable in the character. Christoph Waltz however, is wasted. When you consider his acting ability and the silliness of adding the familiar character of Blofeld, it doesn't come off as menacing but more like a stupid joke. *Spectre* is the weakest of the Daniel Craig Bond movies. Instead of adding something new or innovative to the series it wastes time taking steps backwards for fan service. If you are a big fan of the series I imagine you are going to watch it regardless, but it is disappointing. It is predictable and neuters the James Bond character.

Split

Split is a thriller from director M. Night Shyamalan. While many of his films have been, arguably, hit or miss, Split is a very good and tense movie. The film builds tension in amazing scenes and the acting is incredibly entertaining. It focuses on a simple idea and makes a strong story based around that concept without relying on plot twists in a vain attempt to shock audiences.

Split tells the story about three girls who were kidnapped from a birthday party by a man with 23 different personalities. The man has them trapped in a small room and interacts with them in his various personas. The girls try to find a way to escape and at the same time deal with the insane person and the coming of a new personality that promises to murder them all in horrible ways.

James McAvoy and Anya Taylor-Joy do an amazing job. McAvoy shows audiences an amazing display of his skills as he becomes various characters at the drop of a hat. Anya Taylor-Joy embodies the theme of a broken person. Both characters are fascinating and have a depth to their tragic nature and the fact that they are made exceptional through their suffering.

If there are any complaints there are some small nitpicking issues that fairly minor. The movie is very good but if it were up to me I would have cut the very final scene before the credits. It adds a silly connection to the Unbreakable universe that is unnecessary and really adds nothing to the movie except for a strange change in tone that is unwarranted.

Split is a creepy and fun return to form for Shyamalan. The acting is solid and the story is remarkably subtle in its buildup to terror. The movie does its job well and with the exception of the final few minutes it will keep you entertained and at the edge of your seat. If you were a fan of any of this director's past films, or enjoy a good thriller, Split is certainly worth checking out.

Star Wars: The Force Awakens

The Star Wars movies evoke feelings of nostalgia for most of us. When I first heard a new movie was coming out I thought, "How can they make a new story that will be sentimental for fans while at the same time touching the nerve of nostalgia without crossing the line to just fan-service." It is obvious that J.J. Abrams is clearly a true fan. This movie is like watching a fan given reign to make what they feel would be a more grown up Star Wars movie.

Set about thirty years after the Return of the Jedi, Luke has gone into hiding. The Empire has become the First Order. Poe Dameron, played by Oscar Isaac, gets information on Luke Skywalker's location on the desert planet of Jakku. Poe gives the map to his droid, BB-8. BB-8 escapes and makes friends with a scavenger girl named Rey. Together they must find a way off the planet in order to get the map to the Resistance.

The movie is beautiful and the mixture of CGI and practical effects is seamless. The acting is solid and the new heroes, Rey, Finn, and Poe are all fascinating and well-played characters that are a delight to watch and acted superbly. The action scenes are thrilling and the nostalgic cameos are used like a spice in a perfectly cooked dish.

There were a few welcome changes that I want to acknowledge. For instance, the casting of more female characters made the universe seem much more believable and diverse. It was also shocking to see blood in a Star Wars film. It added a level of darkness never seen before in the franchise. Creating more complex villains was a novel concept that really landed well. Kylo Ren, the film's villain is a fascinating villain that goes from homicidal to petulant. It is interesting to watch the goings on in the life of Stormtrooper, which for the most part have been faceless minions for most of the films.

The Force Awakens is just what the franchise needed. It is Star Wars growing up and taking chances. Audiences are tired of movies playing it safe all the time and the prequels were all safe. You knew who would live and who would die by the end. In this this trilogy anything can happen. It is a great movie that uses silence and every shot to its advantage to tell a wonderful story. See it if you can.

Suicide Squad

Suicide Squad is an interesting concept for a movie and is aesthetically pleasing to the eye, but it is also flawed. The acting is fine but the story is muddled. I can't help but feel that *Suicide Squad* was a good movie that was edited into a much tamer and forgettable film. Still, it is colorful and stylized but without the substance that audiences have come to expect from comic book movies as of late.

In the wake of Superman's death in the film Batman v. Superman: Dawn of Justice, Government official, Amanda Waller, played by Viola Davis, assembles a team of super criminals to do the dirty jobs of the government. She has them implanted with nano-machines that will detonate if they escape or fail their mission. When a rogue magic-user threatens to destroy the world, it is up to the Task Force X to save the day.

The movie has a great soundtrack and is visually appealing. Jared Leto's take on the Joker is fascinating and new. There are a lot of charismatic characters but sadly they are not given much depth. The ones that are focused on mostly are Deadshot, played by Will Smith, and Harley Quinn, played by Margot Robbie. They play their parts well but the story does not give them ample motivation to act as they do. Minor characters are there just to add color to the movie but, like sprinkles on a cupcake, they do nothing but appear as decoration. There are cameos from Ben Affleck and Ezra Miller who appear as Batman and the Flash as if to remind the audience that we are in the same DC Cinematic Universe. It almost seems silly to add them since they could have solved this situation in very quick order; there must have been a superhero day off.

The character of Amanda Waller is portrayed as a character that has contingency plans for contingency plans. Picking crazy people, expert marksmen, and circus freaks to act as a team has so many variables to be believed that she would make the selections she does. The world ending threat is pretty much Waller's fault. So Task Force X is just cleaning up her mess for not thinking things through. There are plot points that go nowhere such as when the prison guard, played by Ike Barinholtz, is confronted by the Joker to get stuff to Harley in prison. He vanishes and we never see if he is killed or dealt with in any way, shape, or form.

None of the "bad guys" seem that bad to be in the position they are in. The exception is Harley Quinn, whose role is literally the wild card. When going to a party a "wild card" can be fun. When creating a group to save the world, the "wild card" is a stupid idea. At one point we find out Captain Boomerang has three consecutive life sentences-for what!? He robbed a diamond exchange and killed his partner. Harley even has her nano-machines disabled at one point and still chooses to remain with the team to fight the big evil. Deadshot is motivated by wanting to not appear bad to his daughter so it is not as if the team consisted of Adolph Hilter, Osama Bin Laden, and the Hamburglar.

Superhero movies lately have spoiled audiences. It seems that people expect something profound from these comic films. Taken at face value, *Suicide Squad* is mind candy, which is entertaining at the very least but adds no nutritional sustenance. It is flawed but tries to add flavor that is sorely needed to a bleak cinematic universe. It is worth renting if you are a fan of the series or comics. I just wouldn't recommend shelling out money to see in the theater. *Suicide Squad* is fun, but not the must-see hit of the summer.

Terminator Genisys

Terminator Genisys is the fifth film of the franchise. First off, I hate this title. Calling it Genisys in this misspelled fashion just looks like what a kid from the 1990s would call "kool." The movie itself takes a nostalgic look back into the old familiar territory of the first film and changes much of the mythos of the series. It is a bold move to basically toss out the content of the previous 2 movies and start a new trilogy.

The end of the war with the machines is nigh and John Connor, played by Jason Clarke, leads the resistance in destroying Skynet. When they discover they sent a Terminator back in time to kill Sarah Connor, played by Emilia Clarke, back in 1984. Kyle Reese, played by Jai Courtney, is sent back in time to protect Sarah, however when he arrives he finds that Sarah isn't the helpless young women he expected to find and she is guarded by a Terminator, played by Arnold Schwarzenegger, which she has affectionately named "Pops."

The acting is fine. Jai Courtney does a good job at playing Kyle Reese but Emilia Clarke is just too cute to come off as tough as Sarah Hamilton did in the role. Arnold Schwarzenegger is entertaining, but he should be, he had four movies to perfect the role. I generally like Jason Clarke but it was as if the filmmakers went out of their way to make John Connor as much of jackass as he was in the other films. At this point I really begin to wonder if this dolt is ever really worth saving.

The story is really complicated if you are new to the franchise. Going back to elements of the past and essentially re-writing history is a novel idea. The action sequences are fun to watch but would have impressed me more using practical effects. The movie basically warns us of how humanity has gotten lost in technology and Skynet will become aware right under our noses.

If you enjoyed Terminator and Terminator 2: Judgment Day this movie will be right up your alley. If you are a stickler for details and wonder how this can fit in with all four films you will be disappointed. Next time they should be bold and make the movie rated R like the good films of the series. It isn't really ground breaking but it is entertaining and will kill a couple of hours. Just be sure to stay until after the credits.

The Anatomy of Monsters

The Anatomy of Monsters is thriller from 2014 and based in Seattle. There are few words that describe this movie as well as amateur. The script is charmless and the cinematography goes hand in hand with the sloppy editing. There is very little to make anyone want to see a movie that is this poorly crafted.

Andrew intends to meet a girl in the bar with the intention of murdering her. He comes across Sarah, played by Tabitha Bastien. When they hit it off they go to a seedy hotel where she gets handcuffed and he wields a knife at her menacingly. At that time she reveals that she is a killer herself and he was a target for her. They then discuss what made them the killers that they are using flashbacks.

It feels like Tabitha Bastien is trying really hard with the material. She might be an okay actress if the project was not something awful. Unfortunately, the script, production and other actors do not do any favors for her and her performance falls flat. She is attempting to carry this movie and there is just not enough support to make anything she does memorable. Andrew is written as a sociopath and you would have to be blind, deaf, and dumb to not notice that this is a guy who looks at women and wonders if he can wear her skin. There is nothing subtle about it.

The filter on the lens seems like it has the Photoshop burn

tool covering the screen. Andrew's knife is clearly not real and you would think that would be an easy prop to get for a film. The blood effects and Foley sounds are poorly done and do not convey any seriousness in their shoddy quality. Even the music does not do any favors for *The Anatomy of Monsters*; there is a near constant techno soundtrack and often the volume is so much that you need to struggle to hear the actors.

The script is awkward. The jokes do not land and the scenes are black holes of wit. For example, a little girl's father has a problem with their family cats disappearing so he says: "I'm not taking out a second mortgage to restock our cat supply." The script does not even agree with what is on screen. When someone says: "You are holding up traffic." It helps to actually have there be traffic in the street. There is also a flashback within a flashback, which comes off as lazy screenwriting.

There is an homage to the movie *Halloween* that adds nothing to the plot. It is as if the writer felt that pop culture references would automatically equal humor. Characters that are supposed to be quirky and charming just come off as creepy and annoying. The makeup effects are all things that could be done by the local high school drama class and the action is lazily done in such a way that the only people that will be pleased by the results will be the actors that can now add "stage combat" to their resumes.

I cannot recommend this movie to anyone beyond the person looking for something in the "How did this get made?" category. It is not particularly well made nor does it seem to have a message of any sort. It is also not a funny movie in any sense of the word. The bizarre framework for the entire love story is truly unentertaining. The entire idea of a serial killer looking to make things work within their daily lives has been done better. Even charismatic killers exist in the forms of *Dexter* and *Henry: Portrait of a Serial Killer.* If there was more time to re-write this script idea and re-edit this movie it may have been salvageable. This is the sort of movie that you might need a palate cleanser after so that you do not lose hope that there are better films out there.

The Arrival

Before he became the punch line to his own set of jokes, Charlie Sheen was considered a serious actor. What better role for a man who acts insane in his daily life than one who acts like a paranoid radio astronomer. The 1996 style of effects are very present in *The Arrival.* A handful of decent practical effects along with strange blurry CG effects that have not aged well.

Radio astronomer Zane Zaminsky, played by Charlie Sheen, has just discovered a radio signal from a star 14 light years from Earth. When he brings it up to his supervisors he is promptly let go for "budget cuts." Zane then starts a one-man crusade against NASA to get his data from the signal to the public. Unfortunately there is a conspiracy afoot involving extraterrestrials with goals of terraforming the Earth for their needs. Zane must watch his step or his life and the lives of the people he tells about the signal are in danger.

Charlie Sheen is great in this movie. He plays paranoid well and he has the charisma to pull off a roll as strange as this. You want him to succeed in his goals because he isn't a

cocky scientist but one that just wants to have the truth revealed. Just because the main character is likeable does not mean others are. For instance, for some reason there is a little urban kid written to follow Zane around named Kiki. He is annoying and honestly nobody outside of the movie *Naked Lunch* should be named Kiki. Zane also has a girlfriend named Char, played by Teri Polo, who should have been named Red Herring.

The story tends to move very slowly towards the conspiracy, giving occasional glimpses of what is behind everything. It becomes a little silly once you find out what is behind everything and you realize that it creates massive holes in logic. For example: Why would aliens that have no qualms about destroying and killing things using their technology use several boxes of scorpions to murder a woman? If aliens could terraform a planet to fit their needs, why wouldn't they find a planet without existing life so that the move would be easier?

The scorpion scene is at least filled with tension and is well shot. In a hotel room a woman is walking about, doing her nightly routine. We, as the audience, see that there are several scorpions in the room and she is narrowly stung several times. The entire time you are wondering when the killing sting will occur. It is very much like the build up before a scene in a *Final Destination* movie. The memorable moments are very few and far between. Some characters you are introduced to only to have them die soon after so they cannot be developed.

The practical effects are fine and show a lot of skills to the filmmakers. Where it gets ridiculous are the CG effects, which look cartoonish and unbelievable and have not aged well. *The Arrival* has the same sort of feel as an episode of *The X-Files*. The alien's ultimate goal of using green house gases to warm the planet for terraforming purposes has an obvious environmental message but is, thankfully, not super preachy about the theme.

The Arrival is not scary. If that is what you are looking for then you are in the wrong ballpark. This movie is more along the lines of a sci-fi conspiracy thriller. It is okay and might be worth seeing as a rental or if you have nothing better on television and it happens to play. The movie is a forgettable part of the alien hype that got lost in the shuffle when *Independence Day* came out the same year. If I want a movie with aliens, conspiracy, and paranoia I would recommend sticking to John Carpenter's *The Thing* or *They Live*.

The Bride

The Bride is a 2016, low-budget, horror movie. While I'm sure it was made with love, it adds nothing new to the genre. The production and acting could use some fine-tuning, but with a bigger budget this movie could've have worked. If this movie were a comedy, I would have enjoyed it a lot more. The underlying idea of the plot is entertaining, but the execution comes off as confusing attempt to make a story that has already been told. The most memorable performance is hidden and is not utilized to its full entertaining potential.

The Bride begins with a scrolling text crawl about a legend of an Apache woman that was raped and killed on her wedding day and rose from the grave to get bloody vengeance. Flash-forward several decades and we meet

Kira and Marco, a couple about to get married. In a bungled kidnapping plot Marco is killed and Kira is raped and murdered. The spirit of the Apache woman that got her revenge allows Kira to rise from her grave to exact revenge on her killers.

The story is very clichéd borrowing heavily from elements of *The Crow* and *I Spit on Your Grave*. The text crawl at the beginning seemed like it would have been a much more entertaining movie by itself. The characters of Kira and Marco have no chemistry and between them arguing over which one of them is "cray-cray" and trying to decipher their accents, it becomes arduous to figure out if they are worth investing in emotionally. As soon as Kira witnesses the death of Marco she shows no emotion to the loss until she rises up from the grave.

At one point Marco gives Kira a set of dog tags in an attempt to be romantic. One of them says, "Fuck it on a bucket" the other says, "you are the air that I want to breathe for the rest of my life." The exposition dump is painfully awkward and the overall plan of the kidnappers is ludicrous. Even the kidnappers themselves are just stereotypes played to a wildly exaggerated way. The ending is baffling making it a very frustrating film.

The effects and the production quality are worse than local commercials. The sound is generally muffled and there is obvious dubbing of the dialogue. The guns don't sound like guns and fire off cartoonish bullets and release painfully fake muzzle flashes that make this production rank right up with amateur high school student movies. There is even a moment when they attempt to show a guy on FaceTime but it is clearly a superimposed video in a static image of a hand holding a smart phone. The ghost of the Apache girl is less realistic than Obi Wan Kenobi's ghost in The *Empire Strikes Back*.

The costumes look like the cast raided a Halloween outlet store. The kills are pretty lackluster despite the gore and some of the scenes seem like they might be tongue in cheek but the tone does not indicate humor. For example when ghoulish avenger Kira gets stabbed by a machete she just takes a tampon, crams it in the wound, then seals the wound in duct tape.

The characters often stumble their lines as if they are just barely off-book, this matches the awkwardness of the unnatural dialogue. Despite the many flaws to this movie, the character playing Harrison is at least entertaining. Lane Townsend chews the scenery like a champ and really falls into the role of a comic book style villain. It is not particularly thrilling as a horror movie but the action can be pretty amusing.

I cannot recommend this movie since it was not my taste. The story is nothing new but there can easily be an audience for this as a possible cult film. There are a lot of elements of *The Crow* and *I Spit on Your Grave,* so if you are interested in the rape-revenge genre I suggest you watch those films first. It is not a particularly well-made movie but it does have the potential to entertain. Give it a try at your peril.

The Carnage Collection

The Carnage Collection attempts to be an anthology of horror stories. Where it fails is that there is usually something that ties it all together in a coherent framework. While *The Carnage Collection* does have a framework, it is a flimsy one that does not have a worthy pay-off for the time spent watching the several lame stories that compose this anthology series.

The story begins with a cable salesman selling a new service to a young man. As he hooks up his new box the young man flips through the channels and the screen is what we are supposedly seeing. The stories consist of the following:
- A killer foul-mouth decorative Santa which kills two brothers.
- A POV shot story of a guy buying drugs. He takes some mysterious drug and hallucinates. The end.
- A lonely guy has sex with his VCR, which comes alive and kills him.
- Two guys go searching for weed and get a text to go to the cemetery where a robed figure gives them weed, which causes them to rot and die.
- A girl draws a picture of a creepy clown, which comes alive and kills the girl's family and two random women in the woods.
- A suicidal man is saved from death constantly by a guardian angel that is actually the angel of death making sure he meets his appointed fate.
- A girl is chased in the woods by a masked killer who kidnaps and brutally tortures her. She then manages to grab his knife and kill her attacker before dying of her wounds.
- A girl with a lot of stuffed animals gets a plush sloth she names Rufio that she believes can talk. Then she proceeds to drug and rape a friend at the urging of the Rufio. She first rapes with a plastic doll, then with a knife. After the rape she kills herself.

All of these stories come together inevitably because the cable man is the devil and apparently he just wanted to kill an average guy by having him watch garbage. Most of these stories seem more like jokes with no punch line.

The acting is abysmal and the people involved seem to be reading off cue cards at times. The camera work is so amateur that it is often hard to tell what is actually happening on screen. It comes off more like someone got their home movie made in to a feature length film. Not that it really matters since the subject material seems to be made to display the bitter opinion the filmmakers have of the world.

The best anthology movies usually make each story something that could easily stand on its own. This movie has sections that are more like commercials in the middle of a fever dream. With eight stories and the framework it feels like the writer just tossed out ideas in a brainstorming session and they filmed it no matter what. The sex and rape scenes might not be realistic but the use of sex toys makes the scenes borderline pornographic at times. That level of exploitation just for shock value is just annoying and tacky.

If you are looking for really good horror anthology movies I recommend *Trick 'r Treat*, *Tales From the Darkside*, and *Creepshow*. There are a few moments that are such as seeing the killer Santa stabbing a guy and realizing the decorative Santa has tape in his fists to hold items. These "so bad it is good" moments are okay at best, but, like a breath of fresh air at a Snoop Dog concert, it is a rare thing. An anthology movie should keep its central theme in mind and remember what it is trying to achieve with each story. *The Carnage Collection* are just ideas that are too underdeveloped for an actual plot with stories that are the equivalent of the aristocrats jokes.

The Curse II: The Bite

The Curse II: The Bite is a movie that must have seemed like a good idea on paper but on screen it is fairly dull. Most of the movie is watching a young couple drive around and talk about how in love they are. The characters are poorly developed and the story is ludicrous. There are a few gory moments that are interesting to watch but it only happens at the last few minutes of the movie so by then it is too little too late.

Lisa and Clark are a young couple traveling across the country. They have a few mishaps involving hundreds of snakes on their travels. One snake climbs into their car and bites Clark in the left hand. The snake was apparently radioactive or something because the bite is slowing transforming Clark's hand into a living snake.

The acting is so-so at best. Nobody acts as if the situation is real. They simply see a guy with a snakebite, acting like a psychopath and figure he is just being a turd and they can shrug it off. At no point is going to the hospital an option until he is forced to go there. By that point he has a living snake on his hand that for some reason goes right for the mouths of his victims.

If there is a redeeming feature to this movie it is that Jamie Farr plays a doctor. At first I was not sure if he would be able to pull off an entertaining role in this movie but sure enough he had a decent amount of charm when he was on-screen. The other character that was trying hard, given the material, was Jill Schoelen as Lisa. She had a much more recognizable role later in her life as the daughter in the movie *The Stepfather*. She actually tries to make the material work.

The pacing is unfortunate. It feels like this movie would have been about 30 minutes long if they simply cut out the filler material like driving over hundreds of snakes in the middle of the road. It added nothing, and besides being odd, it really does not create an atmosphere of horror. The puppets do not even seem to be creative. They are lazily flopped about and it makes me wonder why Curtis has not cut off his own evil hand like Ash in *Evil Dead II*.

I was not sure if they were attempting to make an environmental message at one point telling the audience straight out that the world is blowing up weapons under ground and dumping things all over the environment. It is such a glancing conversation that they could have discussed their favorite host of Mystery Science Theater 3000 and it would have added as much to the movie. I suppose that they wanted the audience to think that the snakes were somehow mutated by the radiation so their bite can do things that are borderline magic to a person.

Even the music choices are lazy. When about to have a sex scene the young lovers, Lisa and Clark, turn on a radio that plays some soft-core porno riff that could have taken 4 minutes on a Casio keyboard to make. There is nothing that differentiates this movie from the many others like it. It just feels like a product of its time that was made to be VHS rental fodder.

The Curse II: The Bite is not scary, it is not entertaining, and it is not funny. At its bare bones it is another movie that tries hard to rip-off the formula that movies like The Wolf Man have perfected. There is nothing clever or overly creative and it comes off as boring with nothing of value. If there were considerable re-writes this movie might have potential but as it is this movie is not anything but a forgettable film.

The Gate II: Trespassers

The Gate II: Trespassers is the 1990 sequel to the 1987 movie *The Gate*, which starred a young Stephen Dorff. This movie follows up with the best friend character, Terry, five years after the events of the first film. Much of the same thematic mood, makeup effects, and stop motion are used in this movie. It is not as creepy as the original but it still a decent follow up that is worth watching.

After the events of the first film Glen and his family have moved away. Terry has many family problems and decides that the only way to fix things is to go back to the gate and summon the demonic powers. While he is doing the ritual two bullies, John and Moe, arrive along with Liz, John's girlfriend, played by Pamela Adlon (nee Segall). Pamela might be familiar for her working with Louis C.K. and her voice work as Bobby Hill in *King of the Hill.* They summon a demonic minion who ends up granting them wishes but it inevitably backfires.

The acting is all very on point. The material has a certain level of seriousness that is met well and handled well without scenery chewing or winking to the audience. The silly aspects of the script are handled well and played seriously which makes the movie a little creepier during the actual dramatic scenes. The characters are charismatic enough that you care about their success and hope that they can correct their mistakes. Pamela Adlon is particularly fun and she plays a teenage girl well. Louis Tripp as Terry has a great look. There is something slightly sinister about his look but at the same time he is very vulnerable.

The stop motion creatures are very cool looking and the makeup is quite gross and well done. The demonic minion is creepy and shows a lot of skill and effort in animating the creature. Much like the original, *The Gate II: Trespassers* shows that there can be horror movies for teens that come to terms with issues like depression, alcoholism, bullies, and death in the family. These are heavy subjects and they are dealt with in a mature manner. This movie has a very upbeat ending like the original and perhaps it is for the best since so many horror films have to end on a down note.

I would have really liked to see more of the monster creatures that existed in the first film. In the last big scene a giant creature threatens the whole family. While you do see other types of demons it would have been interesting to see the scale go bigger no the threat level. The story sometimes has elements of Lovecraft with *The Monkey's Paw* and parts of a campfire story on screen. The ending seems like it tries a little too hard to be a happy ending. Still, the ending does not mar an otherwise entertaining movie filled with fun performances and decent effects.

The Gate II: Trespassers is a good movie that is worth seeing if you enjoyed the first movie or if you are a horror fan in general. If you did not see the previous film then you might get lost in a few of the smaller details but this movie does not linger in those in order to make its own story. It would have been nice to see Glen and his family but this still works. I liked that Terry still had a life that was not all sunshine and roses and the temptation of the power behind the gate drew him back for a second taste. *The Gate* is a series that could probably be due for a remake. It is a fun, original, and creepy movie but I would not mind seeing someone else's interpretation. It is an entertaining film that should be given a chance.

The Hateful Eight

As a Quentin Tarantino fan I went into this film with high expectations. Sadly, my expectations were not met and I feel like this is Tarantino's weakest film to date. Written from a stage reading, *The Hateful Eight* is a "bottle movie" that has very little of Tarantino's usual wit and charm and seems to rely solely on the same old character tropes of his previous films while at the same time attempting to shock the audience.

Sometime after the Civil War a group of eight strangers find themselves in a cabin during a blizzard. One of them is a bounty hunter, played by Kurt Russell, with a captive female criminal, Daisy Domergue, played by Jennifer Jason Leigh. As they begin to reveal who one another are within the cabin they begin to find themselves mixed in a plot to free Daisy. Someone or some people are not who they say they are.

The Hateful Eight has artful shots of the wilderness and some great close-ups that truly make the film beautiful. The films has an amazing score that is incredibly well thought out and uses Ennio Morricone's best abilities to capture the isolation and coldness of the scenes on screen. The look is gritty and the cold howls of the Wyoming wind on screen create chills in the audience.

The story itself is a fairly pedestrian whodunit. There are gaping holes in the logic and the anachronistic language can take a person right out of the film if not careful. The characters are all fairly unlikable save for Kurt Russell and Walton Goggins whose characters seem to have actual dimensions. The first half of the story has very little action but as soon as the second half occurs it is nearly all action and becomes little distracting.

Compared to other movies that have come out recently, this movie is certainly a renter. If you are fan of Tarantino's earlier films you will be disappointed. When better dark Westerns such as *Bone Tomahawk* have come out recently then people have to bring their A-material to the table and not rely on the same stable of actors or gratuitous exploitation, like a black man forcing a white man to fellate him in the freezing cold. At what point do we ask Tarantino: "Is this all you have?" Certainly, he can do more than try to shock audiences with cheap tricks.

The Hobbit: The Battle of Five Armies

The third chapter of The Hobbit trilogy, *The Battle of the Five Armies*, continues the adventure after the events of *The Desolation of Smaug.* If you are a fan of epic battles scenes then this movie will be great for you; if you are expecting a Hobbit movie, it falls short. This chapter is nothing that hasn't been done better in films like *Lord of the Rings: The Two Towers.*

The dragon, Smaug, has gone to Laketown to speak in volumes of napalm to the villagers. The dwarves have taken refuge in the city of Erebor in the Lonely Mountain. They find that they are now sitting on a wealth of gold and treasures. Armies of Orcs and Goblins are on their way and groups of elves, men, and dwarves all want a piece of the dragon hoard.

The movie has a few good things working to its advantage. The acting is decent and the monster designs are pretty nightmarish. Guillermo del Toro's influence is felt in this chapter as the Orcs have terrifying glowing eyes and there are trolls with limbs removed and replaced with weapons as if they were pulled out of a *Hellraiser* film.

The biggest problem with this film is that it is called *The Hobbit* and Bilbo Baggins plays a minor character in his own story. About 90% of this film is about the Humans, Dwarves, Elves, and long battle scenes among them. There are so many padded scenes that this movie could be used as shipping material. Some of the battle scenes are fun to watch but, more often that not, it comes off like a video game cut scene.

This trilogy is the biggest insult to fans of the Lord of the Rings trilogy. It takes a story that could have easily made a single great film and bloats it into three mediocre movies. The characters that are interesting, like Bilbo and Smaug, barely get as much screen time as Thorin or the more annoying Wormtongue stand-in, Alfrid. The attention to detail is not even present in these films. Legolas's eye color changes between scenes in the films. Director Peter Jackson even admitted they forgot to put in his colored contacts several times.

This movie is worth seeing if you are a big fan of the series.

If you are not than you will find other versions of this story that won't take 9 hours to tell. The effects are fairly laughable and the fan-service by adding in characters like Legolas and the new character of Tauriel are just too obviously filler material.

The Human Centipede 3 (Final Sequence)

The Human Centipede 3 is the final movie of director, Tom Six's Human Centipede trilogy. The film takes a major tone shift from the previous movies and goes for a gross-out over-the-top style movie that makes the previous two movies seem like art films. Taking the lead actors from the previous film and giving them new parts in this film does little to add to the charm of this awful movie.

The film begins with a psychotic warden of a prison played by Dieter Laser, getting advice from his accountant played by Laurence R. Harvey. The warden spends a great deal of time torturing inmates and chewing scenery. His accountant suggests to him that the way to cut the costs will be to make a massive 500 person human centipede out of all the prisoners. After consulting with the director of the films, Tom Six, they find a way to make it so that prisoners can easily be removed and replaced in the centipede.

The clever thing about this movie is that it starts with the characters watching the previous films. It is familiar since the second movie begins in a similar fashion. Then the characters are introduced and anything clever about it goes right out the window. At first the warden, Bill Boss, is sort of amusing with how over-the-top Dieter Laser portrays him but it gets old incredibly fast. Laurence R. Harvey, is dressed up like a fat Hitler most of the film, which makes him look ridiculous.

The effects are not anything great. It is certainly a self-aware movie that wants to be funny but fails when it goes out of the way to attempt to gross the audience out. Scenes like boiling water boarding a prisoner, castrating a prisoner, or a dream sequence that involves prisoners cutting into the warden to make a new orifice to rape are purely there for shock value. After two previous movies of unpleasant exploitation this is not new or even shocking.

When it comes to a trilogy like this the mindset should be it to burn out instead of fade away. The casting of Bree Olson and Eric Roberts as minor characters is bizarre and yet forgettable. There is not a real reason to watch this movie unless you are super fan of this series or are an exploitation film fan. In which case, there are a lot better things that you can be watching instead of this.

The Hunger Games: Mockingjay Part 1

The third installment of The Hunger Games films is the weakest of the movies. This movie really did not need to be split into two films. The characters that were interesting in past films are almost non-existent in this chapter. Despite that, the actors do bring in good performances, there just isn't enough to make this a good movie.

After surviving the Quarter Quell, Katniss Everdeen, played by Jennifer Lawrence, finds herself in District 13. She allies herself with the rebels there and she becomes the face of the resistance. Once she figures out the depth of war atrocities by the current President, she begins convincing the other Districts to rise up and fight against the Capitol.

The acting is very good. They touch on many themes of the horrors of war. Jennifer Lawrence does a fine job portraying Katniss. The characters of Haymitch, Effie, and even Johanna are barely in this movie. We see some new talent from people like Natalie Dormer as Cressida, but again, she is underused despite how interesting her character seems.

The movie is long and fairly dull. Where the other films had lots of action, this movie has small moments of action surrounded by loads of filler. The character of Peeta, played by Josh Hutcherson, is painfully annoying because, once again, he must be rescued. He feels like the most useless character in the entire Hunger Games series. The entire government of Panem seems to be incredibly stupid. For example, the President wants to quell a rebellion so he kills nearly everyone in a District. This is the same District that is in charge of mining coal for the whole of Panem. That seems like really poor planning unless they have an alternative energy source immediately lined up.

I cannot recommend this movie. If you are a fan of the rest of the series this would be worth seeing as a rental. It is really weak and they should have just kept the book as one entire film. I am curious as to how this will wrap up, especially with the death of Philip Seymour Hoffman.

The Hunger Games: Mockingjay Part 2

The third and final book of the Hunger Games trilogy, Mockingjay, is okay at best and disappointing at worst. On a positive note, the war scenes are developed and chilling. The acting however, has all the charisma of the sleepwalker going through the motions. The film even commits the cardinal sin of telling rather than showing key plot points.

Katniss Everdeen, played by Jennifer Lawrence, is going up against the capitol of Panem. Deciding that she will be the one to kill President Snow, Katniss joins a ragtag band of misfits specialized to look good for the camera. They must face the war torn districts that look like scenery out of *Band of Brothers* and beware of the new traps that await them in their mission.

This was one of the few times that Josh Hutchinson did a decent acting job. While Hutchinson did a fine job portraying him it is really difficult to like the Peeta character. Even after four movies he is in constant need of rescue. In this movie he kills his own teammate at the first sign of danger, and the chemistry between him and Katniss feels as fake as Jena Malone's shaved head.

There are some compelling shots that really play into the "war is hell" theme. The movie unfortunately feels forced and like they struggled to make it at all. If you saw the other movies then, by all means see this as a rental. On its own it is fairly subpar for the genre. There is very little action, some of the key plot points happen off-screen, and there really is no climax to speak of. This is certainly a weak entrée into the franchise that might have been great if they simply edited the two films into a single movie.

The Last Horror Movie

The Last Horror Movie is a British horror film that seems to straddle the line between original movie and clichéd serial killer film. The good aspects of this movie make it hard to dislike entirely but it also does not shy away from being very familiar to other works of horror. The makeup and effects are great given the small budget. The film has moments that are creepy and even trick beginning, which captivated me early on.

The Last Horror Movie begins as a stereotypical horror film, with bad dialogue and poor acting. As it turns out, this is a video that the viewer supposedly rented and is being taped over. We are introduced to Max, played by Kevin Howarth, who narrates the film with an unnamed cameraman turning it into a found footage video diary. Max stalks and kills people all while narrating to the camera.

Max's attempt to make an intelligent movie about murder is his attempt to make a statement about life in general. The problem is that narrating to the camera about how cheap life can be does not make you Oscar Wilde. There are dozens of movies that seem borrowed from to make this story work. The television show *Dexter* and the movie *American Psycho* both have killers that narrate what they do and they are still charming and likable protagonists. Max wants to come off like a sophisticated Hannibal Lecter but at best he comes off like an acolyte of the philosophy of *Henry: Portrait of a Serial Killer*.

In one scene Max asks one of his friends to be honest to him, and from what I could tell, the friend was absolutely spot on about Max but there was no lesson gained from the story and Max seemed to be after a catharsis that eludes him. The strange thing is that Max does not seem to care. He still will not stop killing and he says that his body count is over 50, which would make him one of the most prolific serial killers in Britain.

Despite the flaws, there are a few things that make this movie really stand out. The effects and the makeup for the killings are really well done. Considering the budget, they do stand out. The problem is that many of the actors are not able to perform the adequate emotions required for terror and death. The story is okay but has some large holes. For example: Max inevitably takes this video and gives it to a video rental place and follows the people that rent it home so they can watch it and he can kill them. What if they do not watch the movie right away? Why doesn't anyone report the video they rented being recorded over with a snuff film? Who returns the video once they are dead? If he is the person returning videos wouldn't that be obvious to investigators.

I understand that the writer wants to make the viewer feel like they will be killed after watching this movie. This gimmick feels like a touch of William Castle, which is creepy and cool in it's own right. Perhaps if we watched him doing these killings more it would be a more effective scare. Instead we watch Max workout and brag to the camera how good of a killer he is. Watching a killer exercise is expected in a movie like American Psycho where it is a narrative on yuppie culture of consumerism but in *The Last Horror Movie* it comes off as silly.

The Last Horror Movie is not a bad movie. It is worth renting if you are looking for something to cleanse the palate between other movies or just want something that is quirky enough to be interesting but doesn't go all out on the scares. The effects are good and the movie is paced well.

As a horror fan this movie is too milquetoast to be memorable, but it is definitely a decent attempt to create a charismatic killer.

The Legend of Wasco

On paper *The Legend of Wasco* sounds like an awful idea for a movie. I'm not sure how anyone would be spooked by this movie unless they are terrified of clowns and copious amounts of balloons. This movie is a satire of horror movies yet the actors play their roles it as straight as they possibly can. The characters are interesting and the dialogue is fairly realistic given the situations. It comes down to the poor technical effects and clear lack of budget that hinder the film.

Tyler and Christy is a young engaged couple who are visited by Christy's brother Byron. Byron and Tyler bond over beers and tell the legend of three murdering clowns that kidnapped the mayor's daughter and raped her. After getting caught by the police they were given backwoods justice and killed, cursing the town upon their deaths. Tyler is a dancing clown for a car wash and Byron takes pictures for the Internet. The social media frenzy resurrects the fiendish killer clowns. As new bodies begin piling up it is now up to Christy, Tyler, and Byron to find a way to kill these clowns from Hell to stop them from killing more people.

For a horror movie the filmmakers seemed to pick an odd subject. Clowns to me, and to a lot of people, are simply not scary. On occasion, when the clowns are approaching some of their victims, a room will be filled with balloons as if that is supposed to be frightening. I think the movie is aware of this because at one time Byron says, "I'm just not scared yet. They are just balloons."

The characters are interesting and well developed. The dialogue between them seems authentic and fits the scenes appropriately. The acting is fair but nothing notable. I would imagine that these kids are the stars of their college improve team but they are a long ways away from becoming award winners of the big screen.

Where the movie falls flat is on a technical aspect. The sound has an echo in almost every room, which is very distracting. There is also the matter of the lighting- several scenes are too dark to see what is happening. Filmmakers need to know that if you are doing a scene in poor lighting you might as well have the lens cap on. Either way you can't see anything.

The music is actually very fitting for the horror genre and sounds reminiscent of many of the John Carpenter films. There are some other scenes that seem to pay homage to other films ranging from *Carnival of Souls* to *Back to the Future*. The fight scenes and the action scenes are fairly lazy. The struggles of a girl about to die could be compared with a tired baby being hauled off to their crib. Another frustration is that kills occur off-screen and the violence is simply implied with a blood splatter.

Considering the homage scenes, some of the meta dialogue, and the use of things like a "knife forged in hell," I cannot help but think that this is a tongue-in-cheek movie which does not take itself too seriously. With that mindset, this movie is quite enjoyable. The fact that the actors play it straight the entire time without making nods to the camera or mugging for forced laughs is commendable. If you are looking for a serious horror film this will certainly disappoint you.

As a satire on the horror genre it might be considered fairly clever. It takes three people with real "adult" problems and places them in a situation that is ridiculous and laughable. The only people that will truly be chilled by this story though, will be those audience members that cannot handle clowns. It really is a shame that the technical problems make this movie worse then it actually is. If it had a bigger budget *The Legend of Wasco* could have been the 2015 version of *Stitches*.

The Magnificent Seven (2016)

The story of *The Magnificent Seven* is nothing new. After Akira Kurosawa made *The Seven Samurai* there came the 1960 American film of *The Magnificent Seven*. In the years that followed there were many movies that copied the basic premise of a band of heroes coming together to face overwhelming odds to protect an oppressed group. Movies like: *The Three Amigos, Blazing Saddles,* and *A Bug's Life* are just a few examples that come to mind. With great acting and a quality director *The Magnificent Seven* was ready for a remake.

A small Western town is under the threat of an evil industrialist, played by Peter Sarsgaard. After he threatens the small farming community a couple of survivors go out in search for some champions to drive off this threat. Seven misfit gunfighters band together to help the farmers. In doing so they teach the farmers how to defend themselves and fight off the opposition.

The acting is great. Ethan Hawk, Denzel Washington, Chris Pratt, and many of the other actors truly encompass the variety of the old West. Haley Bennett, who plays one of the farmers from the small town, is especially sympathetic and impressive to watch. Peter Sarsgaard is a fun villain that captures a lot of the same craziness that made Gary Oldman so entertaining in *Leon: The Professional.*

His motivation makes him seem more like a serious version of Hedley Lamarr from *Blazing Saddles.* As entertaining as his character is, he is not as pitiable as the Eli Wallach performance in the 1960 film.

The story is unique in its own way and keeps the general theme of the original for the most part. It skips much of the exploration into the concept of altruism; however, it does delve deeper into the idea of vengeance. The photography shows great skill as the audience is treated to amazing sunset shots. The director also built a lot of tension up to the big battle. My only complaints are fairly nitpicky. For example: the characters run the gamut of races and that seemed fairly unrealistic. Having a Native American, a Chinese man, a black man, and a Mexican made things seem a bit too modern since the film takes place in 1879. Given the United States history it is fairly difficult to imagine a group this progressive. The other thing is that the town is said to be full of simple farmers, yet there is not a single farm to be seen in the entire film. Not a big deal, just sort of odd.

The Magnificent Seven is a worthy remake of a classic story. The changes give it charm and the characters are brought to life in such a way that it will entertain any fan of the Western genre. The film is well made and the performances are solid. If you have any desire to see it catch it as a matinee or a rental. While not a perfect film it captures the themes of the originals and alters exactly what is needed to make it something unique.

The Martian

Based on the Andy Weir novel of the same name, *The Martian* is a remarkably good film. Top-notch acting and a phenomenal cast make this visually appealing story fascinating to watch. The themes of hope and overcoming adversity are a minority in the science fiction genre. It is hard to not leave the theater with a sense of optimism toward humanity.

The Martian starts off in high gear with a team of astronauts are exploring the alien terrain of Mars. While there, a storm kicks up suddenly and astronaut Mark Watney, played by Matt Damon, is hit by debris and presumed dead. The rest of the crew leaves Mars and soon Mark discovers he is alone on a strange planet. He decides that he will not let himself die on Mars so he begins working to save himself.

Matt Damon is fantastic. He pulls off the charm and wit we have come to expect from him in past roles along with enough pathos to make his dire situation seem very real and the threat of death seem imminent. The rest of the cast is amazing as well and I could spend all day explaining how well they did but instead I will say that at no point did I feel like anybody was phoning it in.

The shots of the Mars landscape are beautiful and the space scenes look very convincing. The theme of hope as the entire globe unites to bring astronaut Watney home is lovely and optimistic. There are moments of humor and the soundtrack favors the disco era but the movie never gets confused with its overall mood. There is a tense overtone of immanent death that is always on the planet Mars since he can never leave without a suit for protection.

If you are a fan of *Moon*, *Silent Running*, or *Castaway*, you will enjoy this movie. It is a lot more hopeful than those movies and shows a more optimistic look at humanity in the face of tragedy. The movie does not dumb itself down but rather seems to bring audiences along with it for the science aspects of the ride. *The Martian* is well paced and is worth seeing if you get the chance.

The Witch

The Witch is a subtle, scary film that fills the viewer with dread the moment it begins. The acting is great, the music is chilling, and the setting is eerie. It is a movie that depends a lot on its nightmarish moods, which creates a slow burn to a haunting conclusion.

The Witch takes place in a Puritan New England colony where a family has recently been banished. The family moves to the edge of a forest and build a small farm. Several months later when the oldest daughter is playing with her infant brother, the baby is taken leaving no trace. They begin to face many obstacles, which point to a witch tormenting them.

The cast gives an amazing performance given the challenges of the script. The dialogue is all 17th century in vernacular, which at times makes the film difficult to understand though it does keep the audience in the movie with the lack of anachronisms. Anya Taylor-Joy is fantastic as the older daughter, Thomasin. The rest of the cast is also very believable and bring a lot of gravitas to the film.

The 17th century New England setting is filled with dread. At no point does the Puritan way of life look appealing or seem to have any relief from the toils and drudgery of their lifestyle. The skies are grey and the clothing drab. Visually it creates a sense of melancholy that builds the story's psychological scares. The music accompanying this setting is chilling and has a nightmarish quality that can be felt in movies like *The Shining* and *It Follows*.

The movie relies on its tone for the scares. There are no jump scares or exploitative gore to cheaply assault the audience. The movie is haunting and will linger long after the film has ended. It is a definite must see for horror movie fans or fans of the psychological thriller genre. The Witch is an impressive movie, which is sure to entertain despite the slow pace of the story.

They Found Hell

When it comes to Syfy original movies you usually have to take them with a grain of salt. Syfy original movies mostly end up in the category of "so bad it's good" but on some level the audience has to respect the fun these movies bring on such a low budget. *They Found Hell* has all the feel of a low budget film with a few better qualities, which make it amusing for the casual viewer.

Several generic college students are experimenting in teleportation technology. An accident occurs which opens a dimensional portal into hell and sucks the students inside.

They must face the monsters and demons of hell in an attempt to escape while their friend and professor attempt to get them back to Earth.

The makeup effects in this movie are colorful and imaginative. It is as if the producers at Syfy recruited the folks from the show *Faceoff* to make these hellish creatures. In addition there were also giant leech puppets that were very creepy looking and led to a very compelling and gory scene where some friends had to use an axe to remove the leeches from a companion's stomach and then cauterize the wound. The sets have an eerie abandoned mood that makes it look as though they were filmed in the ghost town of Pripyat where the Chernobyl disaster occurred.

The acting is fair at best, ranging from high school drama student quality to the scenery chewing "I really need this to make rent." The dialogue is clichéd and really obvious. As soon as the students get to Hell they find a sign with the Dante's Inferno quote, "Abandon all hope all ye who enter here." They also seem to be dabbling in mad science, which is unknown to their own professor since upon finding what they did he says "The fools. What have they done?" The students do not even keep the guise of scientists for long after entering hell and fall quickly into the roles of horror film idiots. They are not curious about their situation and they make wild assumptions.

The CG creatures are not all that great. There are winged beasts and a couple of creatures that look like they were inspired from Lovecraft's Deep Ones. Then there are the CG dogs and plants. I am not sure why they felt the need to make CG dogs when it would have probably been cheaper to use several trained dogs for the stunt and they would look less cartoonish. The same could be said for the moving plants. Considering that *The Evil Dead* had a plant attack back in 1981 it says a lot that people feel the need to use computers now to animate that sort of effect.

They Found Hell does not have a terrible story. It is more like a good idea that was weakened in development. If it had a larger budget or even a few script re-writes, this movie could have been something like *As Above So Below*. As it is, it mostly comes off as a showcase for some neat makeup effects in a creepy situation. It would have helped a lot if the writers spent a little time on character development. I found the college students to be basically characters without personality other than what they look like. When a movie does not care to differentiate between the characters in a horror film then they basically just become meat for the grinder.

If this movie was playing on television and there was nothing to watch, I would watch it. It does a fine job of being creepy using atmosphere and not relying solely on jump scares like so many modern films do these days. While certainly not Oscar-worthy, it will at least entertain and if you are into horror makeup or elaborate horror costumes you should give it try. At the very least it will kill some time if you are looking for something that is a bit different with elements of *As Above So Below*.

Trees

Trees is the 2000 movie that lovingly pays homage to *Jaws* with the tagline "Its bite is worse than its bark." Instead of a killer shark though, a killer tree is on the loose threatening to ruin Memorial Day for a Vermont town. Many of the scenes and lines are almost directly from the movie *Jaws* with some occasional tree puns thrown in for good measure. The movie takes itself seriously, which might be the most fun aspect of the entire film. I have seen *Jaws* parodies and rip-offs before and this movie seems to be one of the only ones made with heart and love of the subject.

Forrest Ranger Mark Cody is investigating a body found in his campground that was apparently killed by a living tree. He wants to close the park during Memorial Day, which is a busy time for the tourist season. The Mayor refuses to close the park and this decision results in more deaths at the hand of the Great White Spruce. Mark Cody enlists the help of botanist Max Cooper and the Lumberjack Squint to kill the killer tree before it can continue to massacre the small camping town.

The acting is genuine. The cast plays it straight the entire time and considering the killer is a tree, they it should be commended. There are not a lot of scenes that are different than the original *Jaws* movie. There is a strange scene where the Squint character has a pancake eating contest with a local bar patron. I guess that was put in there because Lumberjacks stereotypically like pancakes. There is also a flashback story of Max Cooper remembering his kite being eaten by a tree as if he was Charlie Brown. It is as if people live in a universe where tree attacks are a normal thing and this common occurrence is only unique because the attacks are so brutal.

The major difference between *Trees* and *Jaws* is the choice of music. *Jaws* has a simple but iconic score. *Trees* also has a score which is simple but sounds much more like filler instead of a well thought out score. Instead of singing, "Show Me the Way to Go Home," the heroes sing, "Old MacDonald Had a Farm." It is a strange choice that the filmmakers made. It would have also been nice to see more of the killer tree. I am sure they did this because you did not see much of the shark in *Jaws*, however, most of what you actually experience of the tree is the green POV shot from its eyes.

There are extensive outtakes during the credits at the end of the film. This reveals the humor and good nature of the production. The work to make the movie similar is evident and really shows the skills of the filmmakers. The effects and the editing are quick and look like there was actual effort put into making the movie a strong parody. There are a few moments of blood and gore and they are pretty funny since it is like seeing a bucket of blood thrown through the branches of a pine tree.

If you are a fan of *Jaws* you will likely enjoy *Trees*. It is clearly a labor of love and must have had a loyal enough following to warrant a sequel, *Trees II: The Root of All Evil*. The movie has good humor and seems like it was made with the intention to praise their subject and not simply mock it. If you have not seen the original *Jaws* yet you should definitely see that movie first then see *Trees* so that you will be in on the jokes. It is an entertaining movie that had me smiling throughout most of the film. On paper it seems like an incredibly silly idea, but because of the charm of the actors and the skills of the filmmakers, this movie works and is worth checking out.

Vacation (2015)

Normally comedic movies get a pass from a lot of my criticism since comedy, as a genre itself, is incredibly subjective. *Vacation*, considers itself to be apart of a beloved franchise and wants to appear to stand-alone. It fails on both counts. The characters are grating and unlikable and the writing is stale and lifeless.

Grown up Rusty Griswold, played by Ed Helms, decides for a change of pace to take the family on a road trip from Chicago to California to visit Walley World just like his family did when he was a kid. His wife, Debbie, played by Christina Applegate, is unhappy and his sons are two horrible saps. The younger is a foul-mouthed bully while the older is a whiny intellectual who is always mocked. The boys are constantly fighting so he hopes that this trip will bring them all closer as a family.

I struggle to find anything good to say about this movie. It is devoid of originality and the characters feel like charm sponges, draining the scene of any interest or fun that could be had and leaving a husk remaining. The movie actually tells the audience in an off-hand way that this movie is different from the original *Vacation* movie and that this one will stand on its own. That would be clever, if it wasn't an outright lie.

Instead we are given scenes that are taken from the original but are wildly less funny since Ed Helms is not a leading man and his family is comprised of people you don't want to see on screen. Scenes like:
-The Father showing everyone the crappy car's features
- The redneck stealing from the family
- The car having an altercation with a semi-truck
-The dad's angry blow out at the family

-The psychotic meltdown
-The car breakdown in the dessert
-The cute girl next to the car in a red Ferrari
-The misunderstanding at the pool
-The parents trying to make love but being interrupted
-Running at Wally World to the theme from Chariots of Fire
Between this unoriginal garbage is a heaping helping of poop and vomit jokes that would make any middle school student pleased.

Even when characters from the original like Chevy Chase and Beverly D'Angelo show up it is only a grim reminder that we are watching something that doesn't want to try very hard. Maybe this would have worked better had it not had a beloved franchise attached to it. This movie depressed me because I enjoy the original John Hughes characters so much and to see them turned into such losers is really sad.

Vacation is not worth seeing. Watch the original movie. Hell, watch all of the original movies and they are wildly better than this. If it has Cousin Eddie in it, that is an even safer bet. This movie felt like a series of *SNL* throwaway skits. The jokes are obvious and juvenile. It will leave you angry and disappointed and generally you expect more out of your comedic movies.

X-Men: Apocalypse

X-Men Apocalypse is the ninth film in the X-Men franchise. Since X-Men: Days of Future Past essentially retconned the series, the stakes have been raised. The characters were fun and the story was fast paced. The actors bring fine performances for the most part even though there are a few superfluous characters. For a Summer blockbuster it is exactly what to expect from a superhero film.

The first mutant En Sabah Nur has awoken in Egypt. Upon awakening in 1983 he recruits four powerful mutants to act as his four horsemen. Together they intend to destroy the world and remake it where the strong survive and the weak are culled. It is up to Professor Xavier and his X-Men to stop this titanic threat.

The addition of Oscar Issac as the villainous En Sabah Nur was a great choice. Sophie Turner as a young Jean Grey handles the roll with the gravitas it deserves. There are some other characters that seem sort of superfluous to the plot but were seemingly added for fan service- characters like Moira MacTaggart and Wolverine are welcome but not needed for the plot to continue. The actors who were in previous films fall into their respective roll fantastically. The one exception is Jennifer Lawrence, who at times seems to be sleep walking through her role to collect a paycheck.

The effects are fun and the devastation is on scale with some of the greatest Roland Emmerich movies. The fight scenes are entertaining and work well in displaying what these mutants are capable of on a grand scale. The scenes involving Quicksilver are really exciting to watch. At this point a Quicksilver or Magneto movie would be welcome since their characters are so entertaining to watch.

If you are fan of the franchise, this movie is a must see. If you are new to the world of X-Men then I suggest at the very least watching a few of the past movies. *X-Men: Apocalypse* is a great follow up for the series and a great popcorn film to turn off your brain and enjoy. I can only imagine where the new storyline will go as the franchise continues.

PART 2: ESSAYS

Top Ten Movies That Bombed

Movie bombs are not always terrible. By the same token not all good movies do well in the box office. In fact there are quite a few movies that have had reputations for being box office bombs. If the box office were an accurate display of what was good or not many more Oscar winning movies would be chosen by the public over summer blockbusters.

10. Treasure Planet
Budget $140 million
Box office $109.6 million
Disney's *Treasure Planet* is a fun take on the <u>Treasure Island</u> story. Adding a sci-fi theme to the story it melds hand drawn animation with computer animation. The movie is creative and lovely. Maybe the science fiction element scared off folks. Any family with kids should give it a try.

9. Heathers
Budget $2 million
Box office $1.1million
Heathers is a dark and sardonic look at the high school experience. The movie is about school students killing each other so perhaps the subject material was just a bit too harsh for audiences. I certainly couldn't imagine this movie getting greenlit today. If you are a high school senior this is a must watch.

8. Big Trouble in Little China
Budget $20 million
Box office $11.1 million
Director John Carpenter has collaborated with actor Kurt Russell on multiple occasions. This movie is big on laughs

and high on slapstick action. Kurt Russell brings his A-game as reluctant hero, trucker Jack Burton, who gets his truck stolen in Chinatown and must retrieve it from a mystical foe. It is a fun movie that must not have found the right audience.

7. Sunshine
Budget $40 million
Box office $32 million
Sunshine is a suspenseful sci-fi movie about a crew attempting to re-start a dying sun. The cast is great and the story is gripping. My guess is that not a lot of people heard about it because it is considered a British film. This is a worthwhile movie for anyone who enjoys a dark or thought-provoking cinema with a mix of slasher elements for good measure.

6. Highlander
Budget $19 million
Box office $12.9 million
Highlander is a beautiful movie. Full to the brim with lovely landscape shots and decapitating action. I imagine that the constant time shifting between the scenes caused confusion with some folks. Still, this movie is enjoyable, quotable, and has a great soundtrack. See it if you are in the mood for a modern fantasy.

5. Children of Men
Budget $76 million
Box office $70 million
Children of Men tells the story of a dystopian society where children are no longer born. Suddenly a refugee brings hope because she is pregnant. The world that is created is depressing but well constructed and had some impressive

shots and a very memorable chase scene. There are few movies like it but it is worth seeing since the director has since moved onto much bigger scale movies like *Gravity*.

4. Grindhouse
Budget $53 million
Box office $25.4
Two great directors put forth a fantastic movie. Robert Rodriguez and Quentin Tarantino both direct different features and yet *Grindhouse* bombed. Why? My guess is the incredible length of the two films combined with the fake trailers really scared off a lot of people. Three hours was still considered a long sit for 2007. Now it is almost a normal expectation.

3. Ed Wood
Budget $18 million
Box office $5.9
Ed Wood tells the story of a notoriously bad director and his dreams of making movies. It is possibly one of Tim Burton's best films. If there were a couple of reasons this movie didn't do well it would probably be because it was shot in black and white and people don't really know who Ed Wood is.

2. The Iron Giant
Budget $70 million
Box office 31.3 million
The Iron Giant is a fantastic movie. The animation is wonderful, the story is original and the characters are likable. It didn't do well at all in the box-office but has gained a following that is growing and the director Brad Bird has gone on to making many Pixar classics like Ratatouille and The Incredibles. If you are young or old

you should check out *The Iron Giant*.

1. Dredd
Budget $45 million
Box office $41.5
This action packed siege movie caught many by surprise. It has gained a lot of good publicity since coming to DVD but it didn't do well at the box office at all. If I had to guess it would be because people thought it would be a lot like the previous version that Sylvester Stallone starred in. The effects and the script are solid for this movie and it is a lot of fun. If you are an action fan this movie is right up your alley.

If anything this shows that the public as a whole is not always right about the quality of a film. All of these movies are completely worth seeing. The best policy is just using your best judgment. What is popular is not always going to be good and what is good is certainly not always going to be popular.

Movies for Expecting Parents

If you are an expecting parent like Kira and I, you might be in the mood for films that reflect the moods you are going through. For this article I asked my wife, Kira, to assist me by coming up with five movies that she feels are gems for expecting parents and I would do the same.

Ryan's List

5. *A Nightmare on Elm Street 5: The Dream Child* - One of the weaker of the Freddy Krueger films, this one has the unique charm of using an unborn child's dreams for Freddy

to kill his victims. The kills are original and the set pieces are inventive. It is bizarre but also sort of a novel concept for the franchise to go in this direction. Still, it is worthy of watching and certainly worth a mention.

4. *Juno* - Winner of an Academy award for Best Original Screenplay, *Juno* is the story of a young high school girl that becomes pregnant and wants to give the child up for adoption. The dialogue is witty and the situations are both comical and moving. Juno is a very human character and her story arc is fascinating. Both pro-life and pro-choice viewers have embraced the film.

3. *Saved!* - Much like *Juno*, *Saved!* tells the story of a High School girl who becomes pregnant. It is mostly the reactions of her friends and loved ones in the Christian school backdrop that make this an entertaining movie. It is a biting satire on the hypocrisy of churches and the way people ostracize those that are different. For a teen comedy it comes off very genuine and addresses its material with the respect it deserves.

2. *Children of Men* - In a world where all humans are sterile there is very little hope to survive. Theo, played by Clive Owen, finds out there is a refugee woman who is pregnant and he must keep her safe. The movie is incredibly well shot and portrays this dismal future in such a way that you want the characters to overcome the incredible odds they must face. The movie causes a vast amalgam of emotions from horror to a crescendo of hope.

1. *Rosemary's Baby* - This movie is, at its core, about a woman's desire to control her own pregnancy. However it tells it in the guise of a smart psychological thriller.

Rosemary and her husband move into an apartment with some strange neighbors living nearby. After a night of bizarre dreams Rosemary finds she is pregnant. She also becomes increasingly paranoid, as she doesn't know if the threats she faces are real or imagined. It is a classic movie that everyone should see.

Kira's List

5. *Junior* - Arnold Schwarzenegger gets pregnant- 'nuff said. For those of us who love a good fish out of water story, watching Schwarzenegger's character, Alex Hesse, battle nausea, raging hormones, and binge eating is just what the doctor ordered. Sure, you'll need to overlook a majority of the medical anomalies to enjoy this movie, but underneath you'll find its charm and awkward entertainment.

4. *Nine Months* - *Nine Months* is the story of an unmarried couple who find themselves expecting a baby. Rebecca Taylor, played by Julianne Moore, is excited to take on her new role as a mother while Samuel Faulkner, played by Hugh Grant, is not as enthusiastic. Their story is a familiar one with miscommunications that lead to conflict, inevitably ending with understanding and forgiveness. The simple storyline isn't what does it for me though; it's really Tom Arnold that steals the show. His character, Marty, delivers a blunt view on raising children and provides welcomed comic relief. We can't forget Robin Williams who plays a foreign OBGYN with a huge language barrier.

3. *Father of the Bride 2* —The exacerbated George Banks returns as the loveable character you knew him from in the first film, *Father of the Bride*. In the sequel, his quirkiness is escalated as he finds himself simultaneously becoming a

father and grandfather. Steve Martin does a great job portraying a man overcome with happiness for the birth of his first grandchild and overwhelming terror of becoming a father again at such a late time in his life. As an expecting mother, I enjoyed watching two women of wildly different ages grow belly bumps and prepare for impending childbirth.

2. *For Keeps* – This is known as Molly Ringwald's last role in a teen film and one of her more mature roles for sure. Ringwald's character, Darcy, becomes pregnant during her senior year of high school by her boyfriend of the same age, Stan. We watch the couple journey from being teenagers who get married and optimistically assure themselves they are ready to raise a child, to struggling with post-partum depression and threats of divorce. This is a grim look into the reality of high school pregnancy long before MTV exploited the issue.

1. *Fools Rush In* – A one-night stand that leads to a shotgun wedding. This movie delivers Matthew Perry as the awkward, uptight personality we all love. Perry's character, Alex Whitman, is forced out of his comfort zone when he impregnates and marries Isabel Fuentes, played by Salma Hayek. Both characters help each other grow into better people and inevitably win the hearts of their in-laws. Set in Las Vegas, this movie is a fun, over-the-top blend of cultures.

Top Ten Last Words For Movie Characters

Movies have the power to move audiences in hundreds of different ways. When a character meets their end, more often than not, they are given powerful final words.

Sometimes the words are amusing-sometimes sad- but too many to count are quotable and have joined the pop culture lexicon. This leads to what I believe is the top ten best last words for characters in movies.

10. "Abracadabra." - The Prestige
Turn of the century magician, Alfred Borden is arrested for a crime he didn't commit. Through the twists and turns of the story we learn of his rivalry with magician Robert Angier and how he came to be on death row. This leads to him being led to the gallows and saying his famous last words before meeting his death.

9. "We... Are...Groot." - Guardians of the Galaxy
Groot, the tree-man of the space faring group the Guardians of the Galaxy, needs to save the universe from an evil alien creature with destruction on his mind. In an act of bravery he protects the rest of the group from what would otherwise be a fatal explosion. Because his vocabulary is so limited, his words are a testament to how much he regards his new companions.

8. "Is that the best you can do, you pansies?" - Sin City
Said by Marv after being sent to the electric chair. Marv goes on a killing spree to find who killed a woman named Goldie who he is in love with. Marv's thirst for violence, revenge, and primitive justice gets him the killer at the cost of his own life. It takes a couple of rounds of electricity to bring an almost unstoppable hulk like Marv down.

7. "James, earn this...earn it." - Saving Private Ryan
World War II and a squad of men are sent to collect Private James Ryan and send him home. Captain Miller and his men need only to collect Private Ryan, however he

refuses to leave his comrades defending a bridge. This leads to a violent battle where nearly everyone is killed, including Captain Miller who tells Ryan to "Earn this." meaning to be a good man. Private Ryan spends the rest of his life doing so to make the sacrifices of the soldiers worthwhile.

6. "Remember what I said about seein' a light when you die? It ain't true. I can't see a damn thing." – Tombstone

A rival gang of cowboys has shot Morgan Earp. As he lays dying on a pool table he remembers a conversation he had with his brothers about death. He offers his point of view of what it feels like to slip off the mortal coil. This pivotal moment is acted extremely well by Bill Paxton and it brings much of the reckoning on the cowboy's head's for their actions.

5. "Why don't we just…wait here for a little while…see what happens?" – The Thing

After battling a shape-shifting alien in the harsh Antarctic weather, R.J. MacReady is ready to die of exposure. When Childs, another member of the research station shows up unexpectedly, he is unsure if Childs is himself or the monstrous thing as well. Exhausted and letting the cold of Antarctica take him, he has given up the good fight and welcomes whatever may come next.

4. "Clever girl…" - Jurassic Park

Robert Muldoon is hunting the loose velociraptors in Jurassic Park. The dinosaurs show signs of intelligence and he clearly respects their lethal nature as well as their wits. When he thinks he has the drop on one, he aims his gun and is suddenly attacked on the side by a raptor that was using the other to distract him.

3. "Made it, Ma! Top of the World!" - White Heat

Cody Jarrett is a psychopathic criminal with mother issues. After a heist at a chemical plant goes wrong he laughs manically shooting at police and even killing his own surrendering gang members. After shouting his last lines he blows up the chemical tankers he is on creating a massive fireball. Truly an extreme end to an extreme personality.

2. "You fell victim to one of the classic blunders. The most famous is *Never get involved in a land war in Asia*. But only slightly less well known is this: *Never go in against a Sicilian when death is on the line*. - The Princess Bride

Vizzini has kidnapped the Princess Buttercup and has begun a battle of wits with a masked stranger who wants to take her from him. They both have a serving of wine with the goal of inevitably figuring out which goblet contains poison. Vizzini is a Sicilian with a silver tongue and will try to get the masked man to give away where the poison is. After much chatter he laughs in the masked man's face before dying, not realizing that both glasses were poisoned.

1. I've... seen things...you people wouldn't believe. Attack ships on fire off of Orion. I watched C-Beams...glitter in the dark near the Tannhauser Gate. All those moments will be lost... in time...like tears...in the rain. Time to die." - Blade Runner

This is possibly the best last line for a movie character ever. Roy Batty is a replicant and has a limited lifespan of four years. He is close to his expiration date and is being hunted by a police officer trained to kill replicants. All he wants is to live longer because he has seen so much and has so much more he wants to see. It is a great line that thematically fits the movie's theme of the brevity of life. There are many other lines that should also be considered honorable mentions. For example:

"Mein Führer, I can walk!"- Dr. Strangelove from *Dr. Strangelove or How I Learned to Stop Worrying and Love the Bomb*

"I can't lie to you about your chances... but, you have my sympathies." – Ash from *Alien*

"What is your major malfunction, numbnuts? Didn't mommy and daddy show you enough attention when you were a child?" - Gunnery Sergeant Hartman from *Full Metal Jacket*

"You can't win, Darth. If you strike me down, I shall become more powerful than you can possibly imagine." – Obi Wan Kenobi from *Star Wars: A New Hope*

Even though these characters may die on-screen, their iconic last lines ensure they won't soon die out in our memories. With great writing and witty lines that have been added to the pop-culture lexicon, it is certain that we will be quoting these moments for years to come.

The Top Ten Most Memorable Movie Meals

Movies can be incredibly memorable experiences. Even things as simple as meal times can often be memorable. Some are funny, some are terrifying, and others are simply visually appealing. When it comes to the most extraordinary meal scenes, often it is not even a matter of eating.

10. *The Dark Crystal* – Skeksis Dinner: The bizarre and evil looking Skeksis are in control of the Dark Crystal. As they gather, they eat a bizarre meal with utensils that would otherwise be alien to a human. Still, the fantastic creatures, developed by Henson studios, have their own mannerisms that are fascinating to watch. At times they move with deliberate ease and others with animalistic ferocity chasing little creatures across the table.

9. *Pulp Fiction* – Five-dollar shake: Vincent Vega and Mia Wallace go to Jack Rabbit Slim's for dinner. While ordering their 50s themed food from a Buddy Holly impersonator, Mia orders a five-dollar shake. This leads to a humorous back and forth about the shake and how good it must be to be worth five-dollars. It is a great sample of Tarantino dialogue.

8. *Inglorious Basterds* – Wait for cream: Yet another Tarantino film, this meal doesn't build on humor but rather on tension. Jewish French cinema owner, Shosanna is seated next to Nazi Jew hunter, Col. Hans Landa. Shosanna knows that Col. Landa is the Nazi that killed her family the whole time we watch them eat their meal the audience must wonder if Col. Landa recognizes Shosanna. The tension is high and it is seen on the actor's face the entire scene.

7. *Animal House* – Food fight: John Belushi as Bluto comes into the dining hall of Faber college. He sits next to some rival fraternity members. After putting some mashed potatoes in his mouth he does his impression of a zit. This causes chaos to ensue ending with a massive food fight in the dining hall. It is spirited and fun in a way that only Belushi can bring to the table.

6. *Oldboy* – Live octopus: After being released from a cell, Dae-su Oh goes into a sushi restaurant. Looking for hints as to why he was imprisoned for 15 years. He orders a live octopus. As the sushi chef watches, he violently tears into the octopus and devours it. It is a brutal scene that is memorable and disturbing.

5. *Hannibal* – Brains tartare: This movie is silly and this scene is no less funny. Hannibal Lecter has knocked out F.B.I. agents Paul Krendler and Clarice Starling. Hannibal numbs Paul with a mass of painkillers and then he cuts his skull off and proceeds to cook, eat, and feed Paul his own brains. It is made funnier by the acting of Ray Liotta as Paul, who acts like he is an obnoxious drunk.

4. *Indiana Jones and the Temple of Doom* – Cultural differences: While investigating a Thuggee cult at a young Maharajah's palace, Indiana Jones, Short Round and Willie Scott take part in a banquet. The food is filled with things like, snake surprise, giant beetles, and chilled monkey brains. It is a disgusting but memorable moment that probably set back Indian culture quite a bit.

3. *Salo, or the 120 Days of Sodom* – Coprophagia: Salo is not a movie for the faint of heart. A group of Italian Fascists kidnap several young men and women and subject them to rape, torture, and depraved sex acts that would not even be allowed in Nevada. What makes this memorable is when the Fascists serve their victims plates of human feces to eat. The whole movie is a depressing movie that is unsettling to a unique degree.

2. *The Texas Chainsaw Massacre* – Sadistic family dinner:

While traveling in rural Texas, Sally is captured by an insane, cannibalistic family. She is tied to a chair and forced to watch as the crazed family eats around her. Her screams are met with mocking laughter and her pleas are met with apathy. It is a scene that has be imitated many times but still holds up for how distressing the dinner feels.

1. *Alien* – Breakfast surprise: After an alien creature attaches to crewmember Kane's face it is a mystery what will happen. The alien seems to die and fall off him leaving Kane able to wake up and start taking to his fellow crewmates. They all partake of a meal when suddenly Kane begins to suffer seizures. Suddenly, a young alien bursts out of Kane's chest. It screeches then runs away leaving a trail of gore. This scene has permanently become the scene that has tattooed itself as the most memorable meal moment.

The Top Ten Most Memorable Musical Moments In Movies

Music is an important part of film- so much so that often a single perfect song choice on the soundtrack becomes an extraordinary pop culture moment in itself. This is even more impressive given the genres of the movies in these lists do not include musicals. This list encompasses what I believe captures that element of a perfect song placement in a film. It is difficult to do, but when it is done correctly it makes a moment for the ages.

10. Beetlejuice – Day-O (Banana Boat song)
A group of yuppies are enjoying their dinner in their haunted house. Out of nowhere and apropos of nothing, the hostess begins singing Harry Belafonte's song "Day-O." She seems possessed as do the rest of the guests

judging by their reactions, dancing and lip-syncing to the song. The reaction the ghost couple wanted of scaring the yuppie Deetz family out of their old home does not quite work out as planned which forces them to call upon the bio-exorcist, Beetlejuice.

9. Reservoir Dogs – Stuck In The Middle With You

After a diamond heist gets violent, Mr. Blonde captures a young police officer. As he turns on the radio "Stuck In The Middle With You" comes on and we witness Mr. Blonde sadistically torture the officer while smiling, dancing and making wise cracks. It is a tense moment made memorable in the contrast to the upbeat song.

8. Risky Business – Old Time Rock And Roll

What is a young teenager to do when his parents are out of town? Open up a brothel in his home of course. However, Joel Goodson starts his fun on a much lighter note. He gets drunk and dances around in his underwear to the Bob Seger classic "Old Time Rock And Roll." It is a memorable scene that predicts the behavior that will cause the events that unfold in the film.

7. The Graduate –The Sounds Of Silence

Benjamin Braddock has just swooped into Elaine's wedding and stolen the bride. It is an impulsive, and somewhat romantic moment. As the two board a bus they stare off into space and Simon and Garfunkel's "The Sounds Of Silence" play in the background. It leaves the audience with an unsure feeling about the young lovers. Do they regret their impulsive decisions? We don't know. The ambiguity is felt in the haunting lyrics.

6. Easy Rider – Born To Be Wild

As Peter Fonda and Dennis Hopper cruise down the road in their choppers at the beginning of this film. Steppenwolf's "Born To Be Wild" plays. The road movie takes them on many adventures through the counter-culture of the American 1960s. The song choices is perfect since it underlines how these men live to be free and are like the cowboys of their generation. Riding the road and meeting people that make up America for good or ill.

5. Apocalypse Now – The End
Apocalypse Now is a dark and nihilistic film about the Vietnam War. Captain Willard played by Martin Sheen, flashbacks to helicopters dropping napalm in the jungle. All juxtaposed with him sweating in a crappy hotel room thinking about his new mission to kill Colonel Kurtz who has gone insane. Listening to this song and seeing the images that director Francis Coppola has chosen puts the audience in a dark and depressing mood.

4. Rocky III – Eye Of The Tiger
In the third Rocky film Rocky has lost a title match against Clubber Lang. His trainer Mickey has passed away and former opponent Apollo Creed has agreed to train him. According to Apollo, Rocky has lost his edge that he had when they first fought. It was the eye of the tiger. The song worked as a perfect fight song for Rocky Balboa. It pumps you up and, for lack of better terms, brings out the tiger in you.

3. Almost Famous – Tiny Dancer
While following the fictitious band Stillwater for Rolling Stone magazine, young William Miller feels over-his-head. While the band's bus is driving away from a house party. The mood is somewhat melancholy until Elton John's

"Tiny Dancer" comes on. Soon everyone in the bus is singing along with the lyrics and spirits are lifted.

2. Wayne's World – Bohemian Rhapsody

As *Wayne's World* begins we are introduced to Wayne, Garth, and their friends. As they drive down the road Wayne snaps in a tape of Queen's Bohemian Rhapsody. Suddenly the car erupts into operatic song as they sing along with the tape. It is a funny and memorable moment that wins the crowd from the start and lead to so many kids in my class learning the lyrics so that they could do the same.

1. Saturday Night Fever – Stayin' Alive

A dark story of New York's disco scene in the 1970s there are few more iconic moments in film than Tony Manero strutting down the street with a paint can while the Bee Gee's sing "Stayin' Alive." The movie itself is nihilistic and disillusioning but that moment has been so ingrained in pop culture that it has been parodied countless times.

Honorable Mentions

American Psycho – Hip To Be Square

Patrick Bateman plans on killing Paul Allen because he has a better business card and can get into exclusive restaurants. Patrick has prepped his living room with newspaper and donned a raincoat. In order to cover the noise of the murder he plays the Huey Lewis and the News song "Hip To Be Square." It is a darkly funny moment that is becomes memorable in the sheer gory nature of the horrific scene.

An American Werewolf In London – Blue Moon

A werewolf has recently bitten David Kessler. On the night of a full moon he is bored and roaming around his love interests apartment. As night comes "Blue Moon" begins to play and David falls to the ground and painfully transforms into a werewolf. The contrast in the calm music and the horrific turn of events transpiring make the scene somewhat humorous and completely unforgettable.

The Big Lebowski – Just Dropped In (To See What Condition My Condition Was In)

During a dream sequence The Dude envisions himself in a porno titled Gutterballs while the Kenny Rogers song "Just Dropped In (To See What Condition My Condition Was In)" plays in the background. The dream features many of the characters The Dude has come across in his neo-noir adventure however he doesn't really gain any new knowledge from the dream. It is a funny moment that will go through your mind whenever you hear the song.

Dr. Strangelove: Or How I Learned to Stop Worrying And Love The Bomb – We'll Meet Again

As the atomic bombs drop and the mushroom clouds flourish the Vera Miles song "We'll Meet Again" plays in the background. It is a moment of juxtaposing sweet farewells and fiery death. Director Stanley Kubrick truly had a dark sense of humor that translated well to film.

Many movies have notable songs that stick in the public consciousness. These songs have an almost mnemonic ability to remind us of the movies. Perhaps that is the power of the film to cement that into our memory. Even so it has lead to greatly entertaining hours of joy, fear, sadness, and anger as we can to connect the songs with these stories. Hopefully, there will be many more great moments to come in future films.

Top 10 Bottle Movies

A bottle movie is a movie that takes place in mostly one location. It creates a feeling of claustrophobia and unease, which makes the movie all the more fascinating. Often they are the films that are based off plays. There have been many movies that can be considered bottle movies. Here are a few that are my personal favorites:

10. Devil – The M. Night Shyamalan film where five strangers are trapped in an elevator and one of them is the Devil. There are moments that are cheesy but it is still written like a creepy episode of *The Twilight Zone*. The really eerie parts are that you have no idea what will happen to these people when the elevator lights begin to flicker.

9. Frozen – Not the Disney cartoon but rather the 2010 film of the same name. Three friends go to a ski resort and soon find themselves stranded on a ski lift. Stuck with the prospects of freezing to death or the facing the possibilities of the dangers of falling below, each much make a crucial choice. The cold isolation makes this movie worth while as well as the fun dialogue between the three friends.

8. Buried – An American civilian working as a truck driver in Iraq is kidnapped and buried alive. The entire movie is shot within the coffin where the driver, played by Ryan Reynolds, calls his friends and family in an attempt to save himself. It is an impressive movie and is possibly one of Ryan Reynolds' best acting to date. The suspense is very real as you hope his character can find safety.

7. Open Water – This is a little different for a bottle

movie. Instead of being trapped somewhere confining they are trapped in a wide-open space where there is literally nowhere else for them to go. Based off the chilling true story, a couple is left behind by their scuba group and are stranded in the open ocean. If you ever feared the ocean before, this movie will make things all the more scary.

6. Identity – Much like the Agatha Christie novel <u>And Then There Were None</u>, *Identity* is a whodunit set, for the most part, in a cheap Nevada motel. The cast is a lot of fun and the psychological thriller aspects of it all make this movie incredibly entertaining. It is a smart movie that I don't want to give away too much of here.

5. Cube – Several people find themselves trapped inside a rotating cube laden with traps. Their personalities clash but each of them is trying their hardest to escape this mysterious capture. It is a strange Canadian film, which is well-acted and fascinating to watch. It also has a bit of *The Twilight Zone* feel at times.

4. **12 Angry Men** – 12 Angry Men tells the story of 12 jurors who argue and discuss a case as one juror goes about establishing reasonable doubt in all the others' minds. It all takes place in the jury room and after enough time you begin to feel to the same frustration in some of these people. It's a provocative movie that is still relevant today.

3. Das Boot – A great movie from the point of view of a Nazi U-boat and its crew. The claustrophobic feeling is taken to a new degree as the U-boat must silently avoid depth charges, torpedo ships, and get back to their base safely. It is a deep movie that covers the horrors of war from a side we don't always look at, the Germans.

2. Bug – A psychological thriller about two lovers who share a mutual insanity the longer they are together. Taking the backdrop of a crappy motel, it gets more and more claustrophobic as they loose themselves to their madness and start covering everything in foil in hopes of thwarting the "bugs" in their skins. The acting is amazing and the mood is chilling and worth seeing.

1. Moon – Moon is the story of a lone man on the Moon harvesting resources with his friendly robot. The moon base and a bit of the moon is all we experience in terms for a set. Still, Sam Rockwell gives an amazing performance as Sam, the man just trying to do his job until he can get home. It's a fantastic movie that has an amazing twist. If you have a chance you really need to give this a watch.

Top Ten Movie Endings

Endings are not always the end of the movie. Sometimes they can mean a new beginning to a franchise or leave the audience with lingering thoughts that haunt long after the final credits. I have compiled a list of some of the movies with the greatest endings. Warning: spoilers ahead.

10. The Howling - News Anchor Karen White, played by Dee Wallace, is investigating a coven of werewolves in the guise of a resort colony. After being bitten she decides to warn the world of the existence of werewolves. She goes on the air and transforms into a wolfman creature and is killed by a shotgun on camera. It is a bold and dark ending to film with great special effects.

9. The Cabinet of Dr. Caligari - A German silent film

from 1920, *The Cabinet of Dr. Caligari* is influential on many future films. It may have even been one of the first films to feature a "twist" ending. After a man is telling his story of a somnambulist under the control of the sinister Dr. Caligari the audience discovers that the man is actually an inmate at an insane asylum and all the characters in his story are either other inmates or doctors. It is a spooky way to end an expressionist piece of cinematic history.

8. Primal Fear - Altar boy Aaron Stampler, played by Edward Norton, is accused of murdering a priest. During the trial it is revealed that he suffers from multiple personality disorder and he is able to use the insanity plea. As it turns out Aaron was making up the entire disorder; he basically gets away with murder. Aaron leaves his lawyer feeling disillusioned and shocked. It is a twisted ending to a dark movie.

7. Rosemary's Baby - After discovering that the tenants inside her New York apartment are Satan worshipers that have been manipulating her to give birth to the antichrist, Rosemary finally comes face to face with her baby. At first she is horrified but then she settles down and decides to be a mother to this creature. This is a great ending to a fantastic psychological thriller.

6. Night of the Living Dead - After surviving an onslaught of ghouls inside of a farmhouse overnight, Ben is completely worn-out. As a militia marches toward the house shooting zombies he emerges to look out the window. As he looks, some of the militia mistake him for one of the undead and shoot Ben dead. It is a shocking and sad ending that hits like an exclamation point at the end of a sentence.

5. Oldboy - After being locked up for 15 years in a solitary room, Oh Dae-su is hunting down the persons responsible for his imprisonment. He discovers that the girl that has become Oh Dae-su's greatest ally and lover during this ordeal is actually his daughter and it was a vast revenge plot to get them together. Not only is this movie a brilliant piece of writing but it is one of the best action movies put to film.

4. Brazil - *Brazil* ends with the protagonist, Sam Lowry, captured by the oppressive government about to be tortured. As he is strapped to the chair he is suddenly rescued and saved by a resistance and ends up with the woman he loves. Turns out that he is still strapped to the chair in the torture room and he is imagining everything. He just slips into his own insanity to escape the torture. It is a brilliant ending to a brilliant movie and it has been copied several times for other movies.

3. Invasion of the Body Snatchers (1978) - So many people have been turned into pod people by the end of the film. As a new day dawns, the protagonist gets up and watches people go about their day-to-day tasks. He spots Nancy, a friend of his, who calls his name revealing that she is not a pod person. He turns and points to her and screeches revealing that he too is a pod person and Nancy is totally alone. This ending is depressing but really makes the movie unique from the predecessor.

2. The Sixth Sense - Child psychologists Dr. Malcolm Crowe, has been helping Cole Sear. Cole is revealed to have the ability to see ghosts. After embracing this gift Malcolm goes home to his wife. When she does not respond to him he realizes that the bullet wound he suffered at the beginning of the film killed him and he is a ghost. This movie is still chilling even knowing the ending and holds up to this day.

1. Planet of the Apes - Astronaut Taylor has landed on a planet where the dominant species are apes. Human are used as pets and cattle. Taylor is able to convince apes of his intelligence and is allowed to go to the forbidden zone. There he discovers the remains of the Statue of Liberty. It turns out Taylor was on Earth all along. This is possibly one of the most mind-blowing moments in cinema. It makes sense since the writer was Rod Serling of Twilight Zone fame.

Honorable Mentions

The Thing (1982)- An alien shapeshifting monster has forced the Antarctic crew to blow up the research facility. With only two crew members left and the burning building dying down in the arctic cold the two men embrace their deaths with a drink in the freezing weather. It is a nihilistic finale, which makes the epic effects laden movie all the more great.

Raiders of the Lost Ark- A source of great power has been taken from the Nazis and is being held by the Americans. When we see what became of the lost ark we see it being boxed up and put in a warehouse with thousands of other similar boxes. This ending is humorous and a smart way to wrap up the film.

Easy Rider- Two men on choppers drive across America. They see some of the good and the bad of being part of the counter culture of 1960s. As they come across some men in a truck they are gunned down in a failed prank. It is a shocking and unexpected way to end the movie.

Sunset Boulevard- A man found dead in a pool tells his story. As we go flash back we get to see the event that lead to his death. This has been repeated in other movies since *Sunset Boulevard*. It is not often that you see a movie where you know what will become of the protagonist, you are just watching the events unfold to see how it all came to be.

Angel Heart- A gumshoe is hired by a man named Louis Cypher to find a man. As it turns out Louis Cypher is the uncreative nickname of the devil that has come to collect a few souls. The movie is truly a dark and seductive piece of film noir.

So many movies have endings that are fantastic. These are only a few that have haunted me over time. If you have a chance you should rent them sometime soon and enjoy. Bask in the fantastic beginnings, middles, and ends and treat yourself to a movie today.

Top Ten Villains We Can Get Behind

Sometimes being a villain can be very complex. At times they are completely right in their justifications and at other times they can be understood for their acts. The more complex the villain is, the more compelling the story. Listed are some of the villains that have motivations that most human beings can relate to.

10. Frankenstein's Monster – Frankenstein
Upon creation, Frankenstein's monster is reviled and

tormented. It is abused and treated more like an abomination than a man. The Monster is not compelled by malicious intent but more a childlike innocence and a desire to find a place to fit in society. When he kills a little girl playing with her it is more like the monster is a child that does not realize the wrong he has committed.

9. Shere Khan – The Jungle Book
Shere Khan is the tiger that is after the "man-cub" Mowgli. His only goal is to kill the boy because he knows inevitably Mowgli will grow up and become a man with a gun. His motivation is basic survival and in that situation where all the animals are sentient you would think they would fall more into his camp than Mowgli's.

8. Walter Peck – Ghostbusters
Walter Peck is the EPA agent that visits the Ghostbusters early into the film. He has legitimate concerns but is dismissed with smartass remarks. He is essentially doing his job and is attempting to protect the environment from unknown technologies. His assumptions are even proven to be right when he enforces the shut down of the Ghostbuster's premises causing a massive explosion.

7. Koba – Dawn of the Planet of the Apes
Koba has a strong hatred of humans that is completely understandable. After being tested on many times by human scientists, he has seen their cruelty first hand. After gaining intelligence he is still very angry with them for his mistreatment. He wants what he thinks is best for the apes and in his mind it means ridding the world of humanity.

6. The Facility – Cabin in the Woods
The Facility works to send a group of college students to

face horrors beyond belief. They control all aspects of the scenario the youngsters face but they have a much bigger scheme that is above them. They are working to sacrifice these kids to ancient gods, which need to be lulled into sleep with the acts of violence. They commit acts of horror for the good of the planet and the safety of humanity.

5. Dad Meiks – Frailty

Dad Meiks seems insane. All signs point out that he is a very prolific serial killer. Once the story is fully revealed, we find out that he can see evil hidden in people. The ones he has murdered are killers themselves and this allows him to use divine powers to act as a hand of vengeance for God. It is an insane twist that changes the entire perspective of the story.

4. Senator Kelly – X-Men

Senator Kelly wants mutants to register with the government. The movie paints him like a bigot who simply hates mutants because they are different. In actuality, mutants are incredibly dangerous. They can manipulate metal, control minds of hundreds of people at a time, and control the weather- just to name a few. It would be insane to not keep tabs on people that could literally wipe out buildings or bridges with a misplaced eye-roll.

3. General Francis Hummel – The Rock

General Francis Hummel has experienced war first-hand. He has seen his comrades become wounded and die and not receive their compensation from the government. So he takes matters into his own hands, he gets a bio weapon and threatens to destroy San Francisco if $100 million dollars from arms dealers is not transferred to a fund for families of fallen soldiers. That is a lofty and noble goal but one that is misguided as he has no actual intentions to harm the innocents. He made the mistake of surrounding himself with followers that will harm others in order to achieve their goal.

2. Roy Batty – Blade Runner

Roy Batty is a replicant with a four-year lifespan. His motivation is to stay alive and hopefully find a way to lengthen his lifespan. He commits violence and has to be hunted down. In the long run he is just trying to fight of the grim reaper who is chasing at his heels. Roy has seen so much of the universe and very desperately wants to experience more than this predetermined lifespan will allow.

1. Edward Rooney – Ferris Bueller's Day Off

Poor Ed Rooney. He knows that Ferris Bueller is skipping school and he knows that Ferris's parents are idiots. So he takes it upon himself to catch Ferris in the act. Instead of vindication he has various acts of tragedy befall him, including the loss of his car, assault, and a dog attack. Sure he is not a nice man, but he very well might have been driven to being so crazy after trying to stop this kid and basically becoming the kid that cried wolf.

Honorable Mentions

The Borg – Star Trek: First Contact

The Borg has long been a villainous entity on the television show of Star Trek. However, they are not truly villainous. Yes, they go out of their way to conquer species to add to their collective, but that is also their nature. They are more like bees in that respect. You cannot really be upset at a bee for stinging you. It is not doing it out of evil intent. It is simply their nature.

Skynet – Terminator
Humans made Skynet to act as a missile defense system. People had no idea that the program would become self-aware. In a panic they attempt to pull the plug on the program, so Skynet struck back. They killed millions in a nuclear attack and still had to fight off humans that are constantly attempting to destroy the program. Essentially the program is just doing everything in its power to defend its life. It is killing and fighting just to maintain its own existence.

The Wicked Witch of the West – The Wizard of Oz
The Wicked Witch is justified in hating Dorothy. After killing her sister, Dorothy steals the shoes that rightfully belong to the Witch. Yes, Glinda, the good witch has a heavy hand in the killing and looting of the Wicked Witch sister. At what point did Dorothy actively try to apologize or give the ruby slippers back?

Dr. Freeze – Batman and Robin
Take aside the cartoonish effects and bad puns Dr. Freeze has a very intricate motivation. His wife is dying of a disease that requires him to keep her cryogenically frozen until he discovers a cure. He commits crimes in order to keep her alive in the hopes that they will one day be together again. The love of his wife motivates his icy terror over Gotham City.

Dalton Russell – Inside Man
Dalton Russell might be a bank robber but he has reasons for his crimes. By committing the robbery he makes it evident that one of the safety deposit boxes contains clues

that the box holder worked with the Nazis. In a sense his crime is minimal compared to the justice he is attempting to give the victims of the Nazi war criminal.

PART 3: INTERVIEWS

The Wild Mind of Barbie Wilde

Barbie Wilde is probably best known for her role as the female Cenobite in Hellbound: Hellraiser II. With a number of film roles under her belt, she is now tackling the literary world with her first book <u>The Venus Complex</u>. The story centers on serial killer, Michael Friday, and his erotically charged crimes.

The story is a taught thriller that was surprisingly steamy considering the content being so brutal. The characters are complex and dark. The erotic nature of the crimes are very steamy and worth reading. I had the opportunity to correspond with Barbie and talk to her about her book and career.

You were the female Cenobite in *Hellbound: Hellraiser II*. How did you come to get cast in that part?
I think that the producers were looking for people who had some kind of dance or mime training, as the received wisdom at the time was that mime artists were more capable with handling the prosthetic makeup process. I was a classically trained mime, as well as an actress, which is why I think that I was asked to audition.

I met with Tony Randel and we had a chat. I actually knew what the word "Cenobite" meant, which was a plus. (It means a member of an order, normally a religious order.) And so I got the part. Pretty simple, as auditions go!

How long did it take in makeup for that role?
The prosthetic makeup process took four hours to apply

and we needed half an hour to lace me into the Female Cenobite costume. Of course, this doesn't take into account the hours of preparation: the casting of my head so the makeup crew could design and make the prosthetic pieces specifically for my face, makeup tests, costume fittings, etc.

What goes through your mind as a performer bringing a role as a scary as a cenobite to life?
So many things... Spencer Tracy once advised actors to just learn their lines and don't bump into the furniture. (But of course, he was a superb actor who did a hell of a lot more than that on screen.)

The thing about playing the Female Cenobite for me was that the extraordinary makeup really informed my performance. Looking into the mirror for the first time and seeing that blue-skinned, ravaged face, bald head, a pin through my nose, and metal jewelry holding open the bloody wound in my throat really made a strong impression on me. It was an extreme image and it made me feel powerful. Also the way the makeup was glued to my skin made me feel quite claustrophobic, which again, added to the performance in some way. As research, I read Clive Barker's *The Hellbound Heart*, the novella that was the basis for the *Hellraiser* films. The Lead Cenobite in the book was a female, which I found very interesting.

You have interviewed a number of famous musicians during your television hosting days. Who were some of the most memorable to speak with?
John Lydon (AKA Johnny Rotten from the Sex Pistols). He was adorable, totally professional and very funny. He was also game for anything. (I interviewed him in a giant

net for the TV show *Hold Tight.*) Totally at odds with his bad boy image.

Iggy Pop and the B52s were great fun as well. There was also the "Elvis" of British pop, Cliff Richard. We're both big *Star Trek* fans, so we were able to geek out about our favorite TV show.

The film *Grizzly II* was never completed but has garnered a cult following. Have you ever been recognized for your performance in that film despite it not being completed?

Well, I'm recognizable in a few scenes, but the big scenes were when I was on stage as the drummer of an electronica band were all long shots, so you don't see much of me. (Meanwhile, the grizzly bear was feasting on various audience members on the edges of the crowd.)

I think that the *Grizzly II's* cult status is more to do with the fact that very early on in their careers, George Clooney, Laura Dern, and Charlie Sheen played "Red Shirts" who got munched by the bear in the beginning of the film.

What was it like to meet Morcambe and Wise?

They were fabulous. Considering they were icons of British comedy, both Eric and Ernie were very down-to-earth and adorable. I had a lot of fun playing a store mannequin that comes to life and dances with them in their show.

What are some of your favorite films?

Almost too many to mention! Well, recent films that I've liked tremendously and would love to view again are *Interstellar* and *Maps to the Stars*. (I was lucky enough to see *Maps to the Stars* in Toronto and David Cronenberg did a Q&A afterwards.) If I had to list a few more, then: *Sin City*,

The Talented Mr Ripley, Casablanca, The Big Sleep, some films by Hitchcock (*Psycho, Rear Window, North By Northwest, Dial M For Murder*) and any film by Quentin Tarantino.
Favorite horror films would be: *Hellraiser* (of course), *The Haunting* (1963), *The Innocents* (1961), *Audition, The Ring, Sinister, American Mary, The Ninth Gate* and *From Dusk til Dawn*. I also like Sci-fi horror like *Alien, The Day the Earth Stood Still* (1951), *The Invasion of the Body Snatchers* (1956) and *The Thing* (1951 & Carpenter's 1982 version).

You were in *Death Wish 3*. Did you have a chance to meet Charles Bronson?
We met on set and we did some scenes together, but we really didn't have time to chat. His wife, Jill Ireland, was quite ill at the time and every moment that he didn't have to be on set, he was with her.

What got you started studying mime and working with the SHOCK Troupe?
I was in London, England, studying acting, and a friend recommended some mime classes taught by Desmond Jones at the Dance Centre in Covent Garden. I went to some of his classes and eventually was invited to join Desmond's mime troupe, SILENTS. We worked around London in Fringe Theatre venues and our performances culminated in a week long residency at the Arts Theatre Club in Leicester Square. The maestro of mime himself, Marcel Marceau, came to see us, which was pretty cool. My partner at the time, Tim Dry (*Star Wars, Xtro*), and I branched out with a double act and then we were asked to join SHOCK, a mime/dance/music group that also featured Robert Pereno, LA Richards and Carole Caplin.

We ended up signing a record deal with RCA and released a

couple of singles in the 1980s. We also toured a lot, supporting such artists as Gary Numan, Depeche Mode, Ultravox, and Adam and the Ants.

If you could work on any film throughout history, which would you choose?

I would have loved to have been Lauren Bacall in *The Big Sleep*.

What led to the writing of your crime novel *The Venus Complex*?

I've always been fascinated by the psychopathic mind and serial killers. I consider myself quite an empathic individual, so knowing that there are humans out there who seem to be incapable of making emotional connections, who regard the rest of us as sheep, really intrigued me.

What I wanted to do with *The Venus Complex* was to show the serial killer's mindscape, his motivations, his inner turmoil and his twisted sexual fantasies, which I felt hadn't been addressed in most of the serial killer novels that I'd read. That's why I chose to write the book in the first person, which was a bit of a challenge!

Has the reception of your book been positive?

I've been very pleased that *The Venus Complex* has received such fabulous reviews from Rue Morgue, Fangoria, etc. Although my lead character, Art History Professor Michael Friday, starts out as a regular guy, he really spirals down into some seriously murderous behavior and politically incorrect rants at the world. Yet people do seem to relate to him in positive ways. And Fangoria has called me "one of the finest purveyors of erotically charged horror around," which is an amazing accolade.

Michael Friday is a largely unpleasant person with massive anger issues. What drove you to write about a character that seems to have so many problems?
As mentioned before, I find criminal motivations very compelling. Ever since I first found out about serial killers decades ago, I wanted to know what made them tick. There is no one answer to that question, so I felt that I had to explore this kind of character in fiction.

Did you study criminal psychology prior to writing The Venus Complex?
I read 67 books about criminal psychology, forensic techniques, homicide detection manuals, etc. I interviewed a detective from the Manhattan North Police Precinct in NYC, as well as a few forensic psychologists. Also, a friend of mine, who was a professional dominatrix, was very helpful in my research. In fact, her statement to me that her greatest sexual fantasy was to sleep with a serial killer was the inciting incident that kick-started the idea for The Venus Complex.

In your novel, you compare modern civilization to ancient Rome, where people only care for food and entertainment. Is this something you feel as well, or simply the character?
I think that when writing fiction, it's almost as if you're doing an acting job. You have to put yourself in the shoes of your character. You have to think as they would, otherwise you wouldn't be able fool people into believing that the character is real. (Catherine Trammell called this "suspension of disbelief" in another one of my favorite films, *Basic Instinct.*)

I think that Michael got to the point in his life when he was extremely cynical about humans and their motivations. I am a bit cynical, but not as much as he is.

If your novel were turned into a film, whom would you want to play Michael Friday?
I think that Michael Fassbinder would be a fabulous Michael.

Michael blames violence in schools on movies and TV. What are your opinions about violence in the media?
I am totally against censorship, but I do think that parents should take some responsibility for what their children are watching and the effects that really violent shows might have on young minds. However, saying that, I was really disturbed by some sci-fi movies that I watched as a kid and I didn't turn out to be an ax murderer! However, I am not a man. Violence seems to be an easy option for men, young men in particular. You only have to observe what is happening all over the world to wonder whether TV, or movies, or video games don't feed into this adoration of violence. Of course, there are also the viruses of tribalism, "culture" and tradition that feed violence, especially against women.

Michael goes on long rants at times regarding his distaste for religion, pop culture, and greed in politics. Is the character based on anyone in particular?
No, I just made up the character and then let him run with his rants. Although I have to confess, occasionally seeing certain items on the news would spark the inspiration for a "Michael Rant".

Michael is complex - he hates people one minute then

is indifferent to them the next until, finally, he wants to be a "somebody." Why prompted you to make him care about fame and infamy if he is indifferent or hates the people around him?

I just wanted to make Michael as realistic as possible. He is a pain in the ass, funny, contradictory, murderous, stupid, smart, obsessive, infantile, very clever, sometimes yearning for fame and sometimes desiring anonymity. In other words, a fairly typical example of the human race!

<u>The Venus Complex</u> has a strong main character comparable to <u>Catcher in the Rye</u> and the _Dexter_ novels. Both stories contain a smart character that is disgusted by the mendacity and stupidity of those around him. Was that intentional? Did either story influence you in any way?

I read <u>The Catcher in the Rye</u> years ago and it's a wonderful book, but I can't say that it had any direct influence on me. And to be honest, <u>The Venus Complex</u> in first draft form was finished a long time before _Dexter_ hit the TV screens. (It was a bit of a challenge to find a publisher that understood me.) I've never read the _Dexter_ novels, so there wasn't any influence there.

The non-fiction books that made the biggest impression on me were <u>The Order of the Assassins</u> and <u>The Criminal History of Mankind</u> – both by Colin Wilson. As far as fiction is concerned, I loved <u>The Red Dragon</u> by Thomas Harris because he really delved into the character of the serial killer, Francis Dolarhyde, in that book. I've always been more interested in the whydunnit, than the whodunit. Fiction authors that I admire are: Shirley Jackson (<u>The Lottery</u>, <u>_The Haunting of Hill House_</u>), Patricia Highsmith (<u>The Talented Mr Ripley</u>, <u>Strangers on a Train</u>), Dashiell

Hammett (The Thin Man), Raymond Chandler (The Big Sleep) and Clive Barker (The Hellbound Heart, Cabal, Weaveworld) and finally Ernest Hemingway for his economical, muscular writing style.

Is this the last we'll hear of this particular killer, or will his tales continue in further stories?
People keep asking me about a sequel. I'm giving it some thought...

What projects are you currently working on?
I'm writing a screenplay based on one of my short horror stories, "Zulu Zombies". "Zulu Zombies" was published late last year in the *Bestiarum Vocabulum* anthology by Western Legends Press and then reprinted in Fangoria's Gorezone #29.

I'm also putting together an illustrated collection of my short horror stories, as well as co-writing a musical drama for stage and screen.

Barbie Wilde can be found on the following:
Website: www.barbiewilde.com
Facebook: www.facebook.com/BarbieWildeAuthorActress
Twitter: @barbiewilde
Youtube: www.youtube.com/barbiewilde

Getting to Know Catherine Mary Stewart

Actress Catherine Mary Stewart has had a film career that has spanned over 30 years. She has worked with numerous stars in both television and film during her roles in such film as: *The Apple, Night of the Comet, The Last Star Fighter,* and *Weekend at Bernie's* as well as appearing as the original

Kayla Brady on *Days of Our Lives*. I had the opportunity to correspond with Catherine and talk to her about her long and fascinating career in show business.

You're film debut began with the musical *The Apple*. What is your background in song in dance?
I was a dancer before I was an actor. I performed with a professional company in Canada called Synergy. When I graduated from high school, I moved to London, England to continue my dance training. I auditioned for *The Apple* there as a dancer and ended up with the leading role.

The cult status for *The Apple* has grown tremendously as of late. What are your thoughts on this film's upsurge in popularity?
I think people are entertained by the campiness. It was created with the idea that it had a good message, great music, and it was a popular genre at the time. The filmmakers were very serious about making a good movie. The reaction from the audience is similar to that of *Rocky Horror Picture Show*. It is screened all over the country regularly and several times at the prestigious Lincoln Center in New York City.

When you were Kayla Brady in *Days of Our Lives* what was it like to be part of such a tight acting schedule?
Shooting soap operas are the hardest work I've ever done as an actress. There was a lot of dialogue, pressure to do everything in one take, and a very quick schedule. It was difficult, but I worked with incredible professionals who were very helpful.

What was the experience of *The Last Star Fighter* like for you?

The Last Starfighter was a wonderful experience for me. It was the first feature film I worked on in the U.S. Nick Castle was a terrific and supportive director. This was his baby and it truly was a labor of love. Lance Guest and I became good friends and remain so to this day. I think it's a beautiful story. It's also ground breaking in terms of digital special effects. Programs that are the foundation of special effects today were created for this movie.

What was the atmosphere of the set of *Night of the Comet?*

I remember it being sort of "gorilla" filmmaking. It was low budget with a crazy schedule. We shot a lot of nights so places like the shopping mall would be empty. We also shot during Christmas at a time of day when no one was downtown to create a sense that LA was empty. I can't imagine that that would be the case today. The shoot was a lot of fun and a collaborative effort. We were all in it together.

In *Weekend at Bernie's* you are part of the slapstick humor. What was it like to be part of such a zany film?

It was a lot of fun. I love physical comedy. I also get a kick out of the fact that it has such an enduring life. It's become that sort of genre classic.

The Girl Next Door is a disturbing film that most people would be shocked by. What shocks or scares you?

I'm not one for horror movies. They really scare me. I go to movies to be entertained in a happy way. I also love romance, movies with a resounding message of hope. I love to cry in movies.

What was it like to work with Sylvester Stallone as a director?

I had a very small role in *Nighthawks*. It was interesting work opposite Rutger Hauer. He was very intense and kinda scared me. I was still pretty new to the biz, so I found it intimidating. Sylvester Stallone was exactly as you would imagine. He's quite small, very muscular, and charming. He let me stand behind the camera with him while they shot the scene where the department store my character worked in, exploded. That was pretty cool.

What was it like to work with the late Charles Bronson and Christopher Reeve in *The Sea Wolf*?

I love period pieces. I did a lot of research about women of that day in preparation for the role. Charles Bronson had a reputation of being rather stoic and standoffish. I found him to be a very sweet man under that tough exterior. It was an honor to work with him. He and I became good friends until the day he died. I miss him terribly. Christopher Reeve was the consummate actor. He was very serious and I learned a lot from him. His wife had just given birth to their son and they were both on the set with him. I know that he endured some sleepless nights during the shoot with such a young baby there with him, but he never let that affect his performance. For me *The Sea Wolf* was a privilege.

Do you get recognized often for many of roles you've played in your career? If so what would you say is the role you get recognized most for?

I have die-hard fans for *The Last Starfighter*, *Night of the*

Comet, Mischief, and *Weekend at Bernie's.* I did a lot of TV mini-series that were pretty popular such as *Hollywood Wives, Sins,* and of course *Days of our Lives.* I'm still doing lots of TV stuff on Lifetime and Hallmark. I've also made my directing debut, which I LOVE!!!

After such a successful career in Hollywood, do you have any advice for people who are coming into the business?
I would say know the business of the business. There is a good book called <u>Acting as a Business</u> by Brian O'Neil that I think has some useful tips. Stay involved everyday whether it's reading "Backstage Magazine" or taking classes in every area you can think of. Network, network, network and don't be afraid to ask questions and get advice. You would be surprised how happy people are there to help you out. You have nothing to lose and everything to gain.

You have acted in just about every genre of film in your career. Do you have a favorite genre that you feel most in touch with?
One of the best things about this business is getting to live vicariously through the different characters. I love the challenge of discovering who each and every character I play is. It's extremely rewarding. I love the travel. Travel is one of the many fringe benefits of this business.

In another interview you once expressed an interest in directing. What sort of project would you ideally like to work on?
I have a couple of very good scripts that I am working towards directing. The script must touch me in a very poignant way. I must be able to visualize how it plays out in the big picture.

If you could be involved in any movie throughout film history what would it be and why?

I love movies from the 30's and 40's. It was a simpler time in a way, yet the black and white photography was inspiring and the industry was glamorous.

What are some of your favorite movies?

I love everything from *Bambi* to *The Sound of Music* to *Sophie's Choice*. I'm a big fan of foreign films today and/or smaller independent films. There is a level of intelligence and integrity that seems to be missing from many big blockbuster films today.

What is your latest project that you are currently working on?

I am working on a project of my own that I've been developing in hopes to direct.

For more information on Catherine Mary Stewart visit her website at www.catherinemarystewart.com. She can also be found on Twitter @cmsall #CatherineMaryStewart and Facebook: Catherine Mary Stewart